Philadelpia, Pa., Saint Clement's Church

St. Clement's Church Case

a Complete Account of the Proceedings in the Court of Common Pleas for

the County of Philadelphia

Philadelpia, Pa., Saint Clement's Church

St. Clement's Church Case
*a Complete Account of the Proceedings in the Court of Common Pleas for the
County of Philadelphia*

ISBN/EAN: 9783337815929

Printed in Europe, USA, Canada, Australia, Japan

Cover: Foto ©Andreas Hilbeck / pixelio.de

More available books at **www.hansebooks.com**

St. Clement's Church Case.

A COMPLETE ACCOUNT

OF THE

Proceedings in the Court of Common Pleas for the County of Philadelphia.

IN EQUITY.

BEFORE THE HONORABLE JAMES R. LUDLOW,

ONE OF THE JUDGES OF SAID COURT,

TO RESTRAIN THE VESTRY OF

ST. CLEMENT'S CHURCH

FROM DISMISSING THE RECTOR AND ASSISTANT MINISTER WITHOUT A TRIAL,

AND AGAINST THE PROTEST OF THE CONGREGATION OF SAID CHURCH.

TOGETHER WITH AN APPENDIX

CONTAINING STATEMENTS OF SIMILAR CASES IN NEW JERSEY, MICHIGAN, MASSACHUSETTS AND MARYLAND.

"To whom I answered—It is not the manner of the Romans to deliver any man to die, before that he which is accused, have the accusers face to face, and have license to answer for himself concerning the crime laid against him."—Acts xxv., v. 16.

PHILADELPHIA:

BOURQUIN & WELSH,

LAW BOOKSELLERS, PUBLISHERS AND IMPORTERS,

431 WALNUT STREET.

1871.

ST. CLEMENT'S CHURCH CASE.

St. Clement's Church, at the corner of Twentieth and
Cherry streets, in the City of Philadelphia, was organized
and incorporated in the year 1855. The Church building
was erected in the year 1857. Sometime about Easter, 1869,
the Rev. Hermon G. Batterson, D. D., was called to the
church as the Rector, and the Rev. W. H. N. Stewart, LL. D.,
was called as the Assistant Minister. During the winter of
1870–71, differences upon doctrinal matters arose between
the Vestry of the Church and the Clergy, which finally led
to an open rupture. Pamphlets were published on both
sides, and the newspapers were resorted to, as the breach
grew wider. At the annual election for Vestrymen on
Easter Monday (April 10th), 1871, two tickets were presented to the electors—one in favor of the Vestry then in
office, and the other opposed thereto. The announced result
was in favor of the Vestry by a small majority ; but the other
party were not satisfied with this result, and they therefore
commenced proceedings to contest the election. While these
proceedings were pending, the Vestry met on May 3d, 1871,
and passed resolutions dismissing Drs. Batterson and Stewart,
from their offices of Rector and Assistant Minister, and referred the same to the Right Rev. Wm. Bacon Stevens,
Bishop of the Diocese of Pennsylvania, for concurrence. The
same day (May 3d) the resolutions were presented to the
Bishop, and on the next day received his concurrence.
On the same day (May 4th) the Ministers and a number
of their congregation filed their bill of complaint in Court
of Common Pleas of Philadelphia County, for an injunction to restrain the Vestry from dismissing the Ministers
or interfering with them in the performance of the duties
and functions of their offices. The proceedings. in the case
were as follows.

2

In the Court of Common Pleas for the County of Philadelphia.

Of March Term, 1871. *No.* 37.

IN EQUITY.

Between HERMON G. BATTERSON, WILLIAM H. N. STEWART, CHARLES B. SHILLITOE, CHARLES B. SLOAN, SAMUEL RITCHIE, RICHARDSON L. WRIGHT, JR., LEWIS G. BULL, HENRY N. BARNES, J. C. MORRISON, J. DOUGLAS BROWN, JOHN HUGGARD, HENRY L. MARPLE, WILLIAM A. ROLIN, STEPHEN FUGUET, M. MORRIS MARPLE, WALTER H. TILDEN, THOMAS SINEXON, and C. GEDNEY KING, in behalf of themselves and such other members of "The Rector, Church Wardens and Vestrymen of St. Clement's Church, in the City of Philadelphia," as may, upon application to the Court, become parties plaintiff herein, Plaintiffs,

and

HENRY C. THOMPSON, JOHN LAMBERT, HENRY S. LOWBER, P. PEMBERTON MORRIS, HENRY HENDERSON, HENRY NORRIS, GEORGE N. ALLEN, JAMES DOUGHERTY, CHARLES S. PANCOAST, FRANCIS R. ABBOTT, EDWARD BORHEK and T. FRANKLIN COOPER, Defendants.

To the Honorable the Judges of the said Court.

Your orators complain and say :

I. That they are members of "The Rector, Church Wardens and Vestrymen of St. Clement's Church, in the City of Philadelphia," a body politic in the City of Philadelphia, incorporated agreeably to the provisions of the Act of the General Assembly of Pennsylvania, entitled "An Act to confer on certain associations of the citizens of this Commonwealth, the power and immunities of corporations or bodies

politic in law," approved April 6th, 1791, and by the due
performance of all things thereby required. That they are a
part of the congregation of St. Clement's Church aforesaid,
within the city and county of Philadelphia, and that they
have paid for and now hold pews or sittings in the said
church.

That the said corporation belongs to, and that it is under
the authority and regulations of the canons, doctrine, discipline and worship of the Protestant Episcopal Church in
the State of Pennsylvania, and of the Protestant Episcopal
Church in the United States of America.

II. That some of the defendants are members of the said
corporation, and they all claim to have been elected to be
the Vestry of the said Church on 10th April, 1871, and until
1st April, 1872. But in truth and in fact, the said defendants now exercise the said office of Vestry contrary to the
provisions of the Church charter and of the laws of this Commonwealth.

That on the 18th April, 1871, a suggestion (a copy of
which is hereto annexed, as an exhibit) for the writ of *quo
warranto* was filed in the Supreme Court of Pennsylvania,
for the Eastern District, by the Commonwealth, at the relation of Walter H. Tilden and others therein named, praying due process of the law against the defendants herein,
and requiring them to make answer to the said Commonwealth by what warrant they claim to have, use and enjoy
the rights, privileges, liberties, offices and franchises of the
vestry of the said corporation.

That on the day last aforesaid, the writ of *quo warranto*
as prayed was allowed to be issued by Mr. Justice Sharswood.
and the same did then issue, and was made returnable to the
first Monday of May last past.

That the defendants named in the writ of *quo warranto*,
who are also the defendants herein, have appeared in the
Supreme Court by counsel, but they, the defendants, have
not answered, pleaded or demurred to the said suggestion
filed, and the proceedings therein are now pending and undetermined in the said Court.

III. That on or about the first Sunday in March, A. D. 1869, the Rev. H. G. Batterson became and was and from thence continuously hitherto has been and still is duly and regularly settled in St. Clement's Church aforesaid, as the Rector thereof; and that on or about Easter Sunday, A. D. 1869, the Rev. W. H. N. Stewart became and was and from thence continuously hitherto has been and still is duly and regularly settled in the said Church as the Assistant Minister thereof.

That both the Rev. H. G. Batterson and the Rev. W. H. N. Stewart have had Episcopal ordination, and they ever have been and now are in full standing with the Protestant Episcopal Church in the State of Pennsylvania, and in the United States, and recognized as such by the Bishop of the Diocese of Pennsylvania.

And that the Rev. H. G. Batterson has received hitherto a stated salary of $1,000 each year, payable quarterly; and that the Rev. W. H. N. Stewart has received hitherto a stated salary of $500 each year, payable quarterly.

IV. That on the third of May, 1871, all of the defendants, except Charles S. Pancoast, George N. Allen and James Dougherty, assembled in Vestry meeting, at which the Rev. H. G. Batterson, in accordance with the provisions of the By-Laws and the Charter of the corporation, presided.

That at such meeting there were presented for the action of the Vestry, by Henry C. Thompson, the following resolutions, to wit:

Resolved, That with the concurrence of the ecclesiastical authority of the Diocese, the Rev. Hermon G. Batterson, D. D., be and he is hereby dismissed from the Rectorship of St. Clement's Church, such dismissal to take effect upon the concurrence of said authority therein.

Resolved, That with the concurrence of the ecclesiastical authority of the Diocese, the Rev. W. H. N. Stewart, LL. D., be and he is hereby dismissed from the Assistant Ministership of St. Clement's Church, such dismissal to take effect upon the concurrence of said authority therein.

Resolved, That the foregoing resolutions be laid before the ecclesiastical authority of the Diocese, and that Messrs. Lambert and Morris be appointed a Committee for that purpose.

Resolved, That the Secretary be directed to notify the Rev. Drs. Batterson and Stewart of the passage of the foregoing resolutions.

That the Rev. H. G. Batterson declined to entertain any action upon the said resolutions, and he also declined to entertain an appeal from his said decision; whereupon Henry S. Lowber, acting as the Secretary of the meeting, at the request of P. Pemberton Morris, presented the resolutions to the meeting for its action, and they were adopted by all of those present except the Rev. H. G. Batterson, and copies thereof were thereupon sent to the Rev. H. G. Batterson and the Rev. W. H. N. Stewart. The meeting then adjourned to meet at 12 M., on Saturday, the 6th of May, 1871.

And that there has been no presentment whatever against the Rev. H. G. Batterson and the Rev. W. H. N. Stewart, nor has any charge whatever been made against them upon which a hearing has been allowed them.

V. That the plaintiffs charge that the defendants are not now, nor were they at the time of their action upon the said resolutions the legal representatives of the said Church.

That the action upon the said resolutions were irregular and unlawful; and that the Vestry of the corporation aforesaid is wholly without jurisdiction and power to dissolve the connection between the congregation and the Rector and Assistant Minister.

The plaintiffs believe and so charge, as well from the disposition and temper shown in the said action of the defendants, as from their threats, that they intend (pending their efforts to obtain for their action the concurrence mentioned in the resolutions) to prevent by acts of force the exercise by the Rector and Assistant Minister of the functions of their office within St. Clement's Church aforesaid.

VI. The plaintiffs further say:

That the attempted dissolution of the connection between the congregation and the Rector and Assistant Minister is directly in opposition to the wishes of the plaintiffs and of the congregation ; and that if the same be carried out, it will, to the rights of the plaintiffs and to those of the congregation in the church property, and to their rights to their pews and sittings therein, work an irremediable injury ; and that it will imperil and almost destroy the leasing value of the said pews and sittings.

Hence the plaintiffs need equitable relief.

1st. That it may be adjudged and decreed that the plaintiffs are members of the corporation and entitled to all the rights of membership therein, and to the pews and sittings for which they have paid.

That the Rev. H. G. Batterson and the Rev. W. H. N. Stewart are ministers who have been duly and regularly settled, and are now so settled in St. Clement's Church in Philadelphia. And that while they are so settled they are entitled to exercise their office therein and to receive the stated salaries aforesaid.

2d. That the defendants be restrained by injunction special until hearing, and perpetual thereafter, from dissolving the connection between the Rev. H. G. Batterson and the Rev. W. H. N. Stewart and the congregation of St. Clement's Church of Philadelphia ; and that they be so restrained from intermeddling or taking any action therein as a Vestry or as Vestrymen.

3d. That the defendants, their agents and servants, be restrained as aforesaid, from interfering in any way or manner with the exercise by the Rev. H. G. Batterson of his office of Rector, and with the exercise by the Rev. W. H. N. Stewart of his office of Assistant Minister in St. Clement's Church of Philadelphia, before a regular and canonical dissolution of the connection now existing between them and the congregation of the said Church, shall have taken place in accordance with the constitution and canons of the Protestant Episcopal Church in Pennsylvania, and in the United States.

4th. Such other and further relief as the Court may deem proper.

WM. B. ROBINS,
HUNN HANSON,
WM. S. PRICE,
Solicitors for Plaintiffs.

City and County of Philadelphia, ss.:

WALTER H. TILDEN and RICHARDSON L. WRIGHT, Jr., two of the plaintiffs above named, having been duly sworn according to law, say that the statements in the foregoing bill contained, so far as they are within their knowledge, are true, and that as to the other statements they verily believe them to be true.

WALTER H. TILDEN,
RICHARDSON L. WRIGHT, Jr.

Sworn and subscribed before me,
this 4th day of May, 1871.

J. P. DELANEY,
Alderman.

Injunction Affidavit.

HERMON G. BATTERSON, being duly sworn according to law, says:

I. I am the Rector of "The Rector, Church Wardens and Vestrymen of St. Clement's Church in the City of Philadelphia," a corporation which has been duly incorporated in pursuance of the Act of Assembly, approved April 6th, 1791, and of the other parties plaintiff to the above bill, the Rev. William H. N. Stewart, LL.D., is the Assistant Minister, and all the others are members of the congregation of said St. Clement's Church, and have paid for and now hold pews or sittings in said Church; and the said Church is a member of and subject to the canons, doctrine, discipline and worship of the Protestant Episcopal Church in the State of Pennsylvania, and in the United States of America.

II. All of the defendants in this suit (excepting Henry S. Lowber, Henry Henderson and Charles S. Pancoast) are members of said corporation, and all of them claim to be the Vestrymen thereof, by virtue of an election for one year, from April 10th, 1871 : but in truth and in fact the defendants now hold their said office contrary to the provisions of the charter of said Church and the laws of Pennsylvania, as I am advised and believe, and on the eighteenth of April, 1871, an information for a writ of *quo warranto* was filed in the Supreme Court of this Commonwealth at the relation of Walter II. Tilden and others, for the purpose of contesting the election, by virtue of which the defendants assume to act as the Vestrymen of said Church, which said writ of *quo warranto* was duly allowed and issued, and made returnable on the first Monday of May last past; and the defendants have appeared in said Supreme Court by counsel, but have not yet answered, pleaded or demurred to the said information, and the said proceedings are still pending in said Court.

III. I took charge of said Church as the Rector thereof on or about the first Sunday in March, 1869, and Dr. Stewart took charge thereof as the Assistant Minister on or about Easter Sunday, 1869, and both of us since then have been and now are duly settled in said Church as the Rector and Assistant Minister thereof. Both Dr. Stewart and I have had Episcopal ordination, and ever have been and now are in full standing in the Protestant Episcopal Church in the State of Pennsylvania, and the United States of America, and are recognized by the Bishop of the Diocese of Pennsylvania. I receive for my services a salary of $1,000 per annum, and Dr. Stewart receives a salary of $500 per annum.

IV. On May 3d, 1871, all the defendants (except Messrs. Pancoast, Allen and Dougherty) assembled in a Vestry meeting, at which I presided. At that meeting, Henry C. Thompson introduced resolutions dismissing Dr. Stewart and myself from our offices in said Church, and referring the same to the Bishop of the Diocese for his concurrence. I declined to put the question to the meeting, because as I said to them, the right to pass such resolutions was a doubtful one, even when attempted to be exercised by a legally elected Vestry, and that a Vestry whose title was disputed and in litigation, had no right to pass such resolutions. I also de-

clined to entertain an appeal, when Henry S. Lowber, acting
as Secretary of the meeting, at the request of P. Pemberton
Morris, took the vote of the meeting upon said resolutions,
and declared them adopted, and a copy thereof was given to
me. The meeting then adjourned until Saturday, May 6th,
1871, when they will take final action upon said resolutions.

V. There has not been either a presentment or charge
against Dr. Stewart or myself on which a hearing has been
had. I believe from the temper and disposition shown by
the defendants, and from their threats, as reported to me,
that they desire, and will not cease to attempt to sever the
relation between the congregation of St. Clement's Church
and Dr. Stewart and myself, against the wishes and desires
of a majority of the said congregation, and the worshippers
of the said Church; and that the defendants will, if not restrained, strive to prevent Dr. Stewart and myself by acts of
force, from exercising the functions of our said offices.

On May 4th, 1871, the Court (Honorable James R. Ludlow
presiding) granted a preliminary injunction, and issued a
writ in the following form:

[Seal of the Court.] CITY AND COUNTY OF PHILADELPHIA, *ss.*:

THE COMMONWEALTH OF PENNSYLVANIA

To HENRY C. THOMPSON, JOHN LAMBERT, HENRY S. LOWBER,
P. PEMBERTON MORRIS, HENRY HENDERSON, HENRY NORRIS,
GEORGE N. ALLEN, JAMES DOUGHERTY. CHARLES S. PAN-
COAST, FRANCIS R. ABBOTT, EDWARD BORHEK and T. FRANK-
LIN COOPER, Greeting:

Whereas, Hermon G. Batterson, William H. N. Stewart,
Charles B. Shillitoe, Charles B. Sloan, Samuel Ritchie, Rich-
ardson L. Wright, Jr., Lewis G. Bull, Henry N. Barnes, J.
C. Morrison, J. Douglass Brown, John Huggard, Henry L.
Marple, William A. Rolin, Stephen Fuguet, M. Morris Mar-
ple, Walter H. Tilden, Thomas Sinexon, and C. Gedney

14

King, in behalf of themselves and such other members of "The Rector, Church Wardens and Vestrymen of St. Clement's Church, in the City of Philadelphia," as may, upon application to the Court become parties plaintiff therein, lately, that is to say, in the Term of March, 1871, exhibited their bill of complaint before the Honorable the Judges of our Court of Common Pleas for the City and County aforesaid, asking relief touching the matters therein particularly complained of and at length set forth:

Therefore, by the consideration of the Court aforesaid, We command you, the said Henry C. Thompson, and you the said John Lambert, and you the said Henry S. Lowber, and you the said P. Pemberton Morris, and you the said Henry Henderson, and you the said Henry Norris, and you the said George N. Allen, and you the said James Dougherty, and you the said Charles S. Pancoast, and you the said Francis R. Abbott, and you the said Edward Borhek, and you the said T. Franklin Cooper, not to dissolve the connection between the Reverend H. G. Batterson, and the Reverend W. H. N. Stewart, and the Congregation of St. Clement's Church of Philadelphia, and not to intermeddle or take any action therein as a Vestry or as Vestrymen, until the further order of said Court in the premises.

And we command you the said Henry C. Thompson, and you the said John Lambert, and you the said Henry S. Lowber, and you the said P. Pemberton Morris, and you the said Henry Norris, and you the said Henry Henderson, and you the said George N. Allen, and you the said James Dougherty, and you the said Charles S. Pancoast, and you the said Francis R. Abbott, and you the said Edward Borhek, and you the said T. Franklin Cooper, not to interfere in any way or manner with the exercise by the Reverend H. G. Batterson, of his office of Rector, and with the exercise by the Reverend W. H. N. Stewart, of his office of Assistant Minister, in St. Clement's Church in Philadelphia, before a regular and canonical dissolution of the connection now existing between them and the congregation of the said Church shall have taken place, in accordance with the constitution and canons of the Protestant Episcopal Church in Pennsylvania, and in the United States, until the further order of said Court in said premises.

Witness the Honorable JOSEPH ALLISON, LL. D., President of our said Court at Philadelphia, this fourth day of May, A. D. 1871.

R. DONAGAN,
Prothonotary.

The defendants are hereby notified that a special injunction for five days, has been granted this 4th day of May, 1871, and that on May 6th, 1871, at eleven o'clock A. M., a motion will be made to the Court to continue said injunction.

WILLIAM B. ROBINS,
HUNN HANSON,
WILLIAM S. PRICE,
Solicitors for Plaintiffs.

This injunction was continued from time to time, until May 20th, 1871, when the parties appeared by their solicitors, to wit:

MICHAEL ARNOLD, Jr., WILLIAM B. ROBINS, E. HUNN HANSON, and WILLIAM S. PRICE, Esquires, for the plaintiffs; and

GEORGE M. CONARROE, GEORGE W. BIDDLE, and EDWARD OLMSTED, Esquires, for the defendants.

The following affidavits and exhibits were then read on the part of the plaintiffs:

Affidavit of Hermon G. Batterson.

I. The paper marked Exhibit A, is a list of the pew-holders in St. Clement's Church, Philadelphia, as made up from the list last furnished to me by John Lambert, Accounting Warden of said Church, and one of the defendants in this suit, and other credible sources of information. It contains (including Dr. Stewart and myself) 88 names.

II. The paper marked Exhibit B, is a list of the communicants of said Church. It is taken from the records of the Church, and contains 301 names.

III. The paper marked Exhibit C, is a copy of a paper in

my possession signed by the persons whose names appear thereon, and used by their authority, and all of whom are pewholders in said Church. It contains 58 names.

IV. The paper marked Exhibit D, is a copy of papers in my possession, signed by the persons whose names are thereupon, and used by their authority, and all of whom are regular attendants at St. Clement's Church, and 207 of whom are communicants there.

V. The paper marked Exhibit E, is a copy of a paper in my possession, signed by 18 of the votes at the election for Vestrymen of St. Clement's Church on Easter Monday, 1871. At said election 36 votes were received and counted, the announced result being 19 for the defendants and 17 for their opponents.

VI. The paper marked Exhibit F, is a correct statement from the reports of the condition of St. Clement's Church to the Diocesan Convention for 1869, 1870, and 1871.

VII. The pew owners of St. Clement's Church, are the estate of William S. Wilson, deceased, which owns about $40,000 of pews; Henry Henderson, one of the defendants, who took several pews in payment for a debt, and who, although an acting Vestryman of said Church, is neither a voter, attendant, nor communicant thereat; James A. McCrea, who sub-rents his pew, and is a member of and an attendant at St. Mark's Church, and not St. Clement's; John Lambert, Charles S. Pancoast, and Henry Norris, of the defendants, of whom the said Charles S. Pancoast is a member and Vestryman of and attendant at St. Michael's Church, Germantown, and not at St. Clement's; George W. Hunter; and Simon Delbert, who favors the plaintiffs in this suit, and has signed the pew holders' paper (Exhibit C) in favor of Dr. Stewart and myself.

VIII. The printed book marked Exhibit G, is a copy of the Charter and By-Laws of St. Clement's Church.

IX. The Vestry receive the funds paid into said Church for the purposes of paying the expenses thereof, and they have, since Easter Monday, 1871, received a considerable amount of money from pew rents and collections at the services of the Church.

X. When I was called to the Rectorship of St. Clement's Church, there were no terms of tenure stipulated between me and the congregation or Vestry. There was no contract of hiring for a year or for any other period of time, but I received and accepted the call according to the usage of the Protestant Episcopal Church, which I have always understood to be until the connection was dissolved by mutual consent, or until I should be removed for cause shown, and after trial and conviction.

Exhibit A.

A list of the pew holders in St. Clement's Church. (Here follows a list of 88 names, including the ministers.)

Exhibit B.

A list of communicants of St. Clement's Church. (Here follows a list of 301 names.)

Exhibit C.

Whereas, It has been intimated to us that certain prominent members of the Vestry of St. Clement's Church, have signified their desire to bring about a severance of the relation with the present Rector and Assistant Minister : *Therefore,* we, pew holders in St. Clement's Church, do hereby express our entire satisfaction with the ministrations and teachings of the Rector and Assistant Minister, and our hope that the relation may not be severed. (Here follows a list of 58 names.)

Exhibit D.

Whereas, It has been intimated to us that certain prominent members of the Vestry of St. Clement's Church, have signified their desire to bring about a severance of the relation with the present Rector and Assistant Minister :

18

Therefore, we, members of St. Clement's Parish, do hereby express our entire satisfaction with the ministrations and teachings of the Rector and Assistant Minister, and our hope that the relation may not be severed. (Here follows a list of 219 names, of whom 207 are communicants.)

Exhibit E.

For Vestrymen.

Walter H. Tilden,	Charles B. Stewart,
J. Douglass Brown.	Charles B. Sloan,
John Huggard,	William A. Rolin,
Henry N. Barnes,	Elias L. Boudinot,
Samuel Ritchie,	Francis D. Wetherill,
Michael Arnold, Jr.	William S. Johnston.

At the annual election, by the legal voters of St. Clement's Church, in the City of Philadelphia, held according to the charter, on Easter Monday (April 10th), 1871, we, whose names are hereunto annexed, hereby declare that we voted the above ticket:

Walter H. Tilden,	Charles B. Stewart,
J. Douglass Brown,	Delia N. Cozens,
Henry N. Barnes,	Mrs. J. B. Parker,
C. D. Kates.	John C. Morrison,
F. D. Wetherill.	Maria R. Lamb,
M. M. Marple,	Emmeline Griffith,
John L. Kates,	John Penn Brock,
Lewis G. Bull,	B. L. Langstroth,
W. A. Rolin. (My own name excepted.)	

To whom it may Concern.

I hereby declare that at the election for Vestrymen, held at St. Clement's Church, on Easter Monday (April 10th), 1871, I voted, or supposed that I voted the ticket favorable to the Rector.

S. FUGUET.

Easter Tuesday, April 11, 1871.

Exhibit F.

Report of St. Clement's Church, Philadelphia, to the convention of the Diocese, May, 1869.

Communicants 120
Pew rents $2,633 21
Total revenues from all sources $6,604 23

Report of same, May, 1870.

Communicants 274
Pew rents $4,882 36
Total revenues from all sources $20,678 00
(This year there were several extraordinary expenses incurred, which demanded and received liberal contributions from the members of the Church, and some friends not in the Church.)

Report of same, May, 1871.

Communicants 301
Pew rent $4,839 48
Total revenues from all sources, about $13,244 00

Exhibit G.

Charter of St. Clement's Church, Philadelphia.

Whereas, The following named persons, citizens of this Commonwealth, viz., John R. Wilmer, Charles S. Pancoast, John Lambert, George H. Kirkham, Colin Campbell Cooper, J. Dickinson Logan, John Cooke, and George W. Biddle, have, together with other citizens associated for the purpose of worshipping Almighty God according to the faith and discipline of the PROTESTANT EPISCOPAL CHURCH OF THE UNITED STATES OF AMERICA, and have for that purpose formed a congregation in the City of Philadelphia, and are now desirous to be incorporated agreeably to the provisions of the Act of General Assembly of Pennsylvania, entitled " An Act to confer on certain associations of the citizens of this Commonwealth the powers and immunities of corporations or bodies politic in law;" they, therefore, declare the following to be the objects, articles and conditions of their said association, agreeably to which they desire to be incorporated, viz.

ARTICLE I.

The name of the corporation shall be "THE RECTOR, CHURCH WARDENS AND VESTRYMEN OF ST. CLEMENT'S CHURCH, IN THE CITY OF PHILADELPHIA."

ARTICLE II.

This Church acknowledges itself to be a member of, and to belong to the Protestant Episcopal Church in the State of Pennsylvania, and the Protestant Episcopal Church in the United States of America. As such, it accedes to, recognizes and adopts the constitution, canons, doctrine, discipline and worship of the Protestant Episcopal Church in the State of Pennsylvania, and of the Protestant Episcopal Church in the United States of America, and acknowledges their authority accordingly.

Any member of this Church or Corporation who shall disclaim, or refuse conformity to the said authority, shall cease to be a member of this Corporation, and shall not be elected or vote in the election of Vestrymen, or exercise any office or functions in, concerning, or connected with the said Church or Corporation.

ARTICLE III.

The rents and revenues of this Corporation shall be from time to time applied for the maintenance and support of the Rector, Ministers and Officers of the said Church, and in the erection and necessary repairs of the Church and churchyard, and parsonage house, and other houses, which now do, or hereafter shall belong to the said Corporation, and to no other use and purpose whatsoever.

ARTICLE IV.

The said Corporation shall not by deed, fine or recovery, or by any other means, without the assent of the Convention of the Protestant Episcopal Church of the State of Pennsylvania, or of the Standing Committee of the Diocese, previously had and obtained, grant, sell, alien, or otherwise dispose of any lands, messuages, tenements, or hereditaments in them vested, or charge or encumber the same to any person or persons whomsoever; and they shall have the right to take and hold real and personal property: *Provided*, The clear and yearly value or income thereof does not at any time exceed the sum of two thousand dollars.

ARTICLE V.

The Rector of this Church shall be elected by the Church Wardens and Vestrymen, in such manner as the statutes and By-laws shall ordain.

The Vestry of the said Church shall consist of twelve persons, members of the said Church, who shall continue in office for one year, and until others be chosen; and the election of such Vestry shall be made every year, on Easter Monday, by a majority of such members of the said Church as shall appear by the Vestry books to have paid two successive years, immediately preceding the time of such election, for a pew or sitting in the said Church: *Provided*, That until the next Easter Monday, after the expiration of five years from the date of the Charter, members of the said Church, who shall in any way have contributed to the erection of the Church, or to the support of the Rector or Minister thereof, shall be entitled to vote at the election of Vestrymen. *And, provided*, That in case of the failure to elect Vestrymen on that day, the Corporation shall not on that account be dissolved, but the election shall be holden on some other day, in such manner as the By-laws may prescribe.

ARTICLE VI.

No person shall be Rector or Assistant Minister of this Church unless he shall have had Episcopal ordination, and unless he be in full standing with the Protestant Episcopal Church of the State of Pennsylvania, and of the United States, and recognized as such by the Bishop of this Diocese, or in case of vacancy in the Episcopate, by the Standing Committee of the Diocese.

ARTICLE VII.

The said Vestry shall have full power to choose their own officers, and they shall annually, at their first meeting after their election, elect one of their own number, to be one Church Warden, and the Rector for the time being, shall choose another of the said Vestrymen to be the other Church Warden of the said Church. In case of a vacancy in the office of Rector at the time of the election, the other Church Warden shall also be elected by the Vestry, to remain until the election of a Rector or a new election of the Vestry. And during such vacancy, the Church Wardens for the time being, and Vestrymen, shall have the same powers and authorities relating to the disposition of the rents and revenues of the said Corporation, as are hereby vested in the Rector, Church Wardens, and Vestrymen: *Provided always*, That it shall be the duty of the said Church Wardens and Vestrymen to elect another Rector to supply the vacancy as soon as conveniently may be. And said Vestry shall have the power to make By-laws not repugnant to the Constitution and laws of the United States of America, this State, or this Charter.

ARTICLE VIII.

The following named persons to be the Church Wardens and Vestrymen, to continue in office until the election on Easter Monday next, and until others be chosen, viz., John

R. Wilmer, Charles S. Pancoast, John Lambert, George H. Kirkham, Colin Campbell Cooper, J. Dickinson Logan, John Cooke, and George W. Biddle, and in case of vacancy, by resignation or otherwise, such vacancy to be filled by persons chosen by the remaining Vestrymen, and to continue in office until another election shall take place.

JOHN R. WILMER,	J. DICKINSON LOGAN,
JOHN LAMBERT,	JOHN COOKE,
GEORGE H. KIRKHAM,	GEORGE W. BIDDLE,
C. CAMPBELL COOPER,	CHARLES S. PANCOAST.

I certify that I have perused and examined the foregoing instrument of association of the Rector, Church Wardens, and Vestrymen of St. Clement's Church, in the City of Philadelphia, and am of opinion that the objects, articles, and conditions therein set forth and contained are lawful.

THOMAS E. FRANKLIN,
Attorney General.

LANCASTER *May* 30, 1855.

We certify that we have perused and examined the foregoing instrument of association of the Rector, Church Wardens, and Vestrymen of St. Clement's Church, in the City of Philadelphia, and are of opinion that the objects, articles, and conditions therein set forth and contained are lawful.

ELLIS LEWIS,
W. H. LOWRIE,
GEO. W. WOODWARD,
JOHN C. KNOX,
J. S. BLACK.

BEDFORD, *August* 15, 1855.

I, WILLIAM H. MILLER, Prothonotary of the Supreme Court of Pennsylvania for the Middle District, do certify that the foregoing instrument of writing was duly presented to the Judges of the Supreme Court of Pennsylvania, and was by them duly allowed, as appears by their above certificate.

In testimony whereof I have hereunto set my hand and affixed the seal of the said Supreme Court, at Harrisburg, this thirteenth day of September, A. D. 1855.

WILLIAM H. MILLER,
[SEAL.]   *Proth. Sup. Ct.*

The lawfulness of the objects, articles, and conditions of the within Charter of the Rector, Church Wardens, and Vestrymen of St. Clement's Church, in the City of Philadelphia, having been certified to by the Attorney General, and Supreme Court of the State of Pennsylvania, I hereby require the Secretary of State of said Commonwealth to enroll the said Charter at the expense of the applicants.

JAMES POLLOCK.
Sept. 13, A. D. 1855.
EXECUTIVE CHAMBER, HARRISBURG.

SECRETARY'S OFFICE.
Pennsylvania, ss.:

{SEAL}   Enrolled in Charter Book, Volume No. 7, pages 595, 596, 597 and 598.

In testimony whereof I have hereunto set my hand and caused the seal of the Secretary's Office to be affixed, at Harrisburg, this thirteenth day of September, in the year of our Lord one thousand eight hundred and fifty-five.

JOHN M. SULLIVAN,
Dep. Sec'y of the Comm'th.

By-laws of St. Clement's Church, Philadelphia.

Of Vestrymen and the Election of Vestrymen.

SECT. 1. No person shall be eligible to the office of Vestryman, unless he shall have been a worshipper and the renter
of a seat or sittings for two years next preceding his election,
and not in arrears; or the holder of permanent sittings in
the Church at the time of his election : *Provided*, That until
Easter Monday, 1861, all persons who have contributed to
the erection of the Church shall be eligible for election as
Vestrymen.

SECT. 2. The time and place for holding the election, as
provided for in the fifth article of the Charter, shall be announced to the congregation on the Sunday next preceding
the day of the election.

SECT. 3. The Vestry shall choose two pew-holders, one of
whom shall be a Vestryman, to be judges of the election,
and shall cause them to be notified in due time of their appointment. In case the judges so appointed should neglect
to act, then the Wardens shall make a new appointment, or
if not convenient at the time to do so, act themselves as
judges of the election.

SECT. 4. It shall be the duty of the judges to open the
polls at twelve o'clock M. at the place specified for the election of Vestrymen, in conformity with the Charter and By-
laws of the Corporation, and to close the same at two o'clock
P. M., unless the said judges shall deem it proper to continue
them open longer. At the close of the polls the judges shall
count the votes, and thereupon notify, or cause to be notified,
each of the candidates elected, to attend a meeting of the

Vestry to be held on the next day following the election, at an hour named in the notice, for the purpose of organizing: to which meeting the judges shall make their official return. in writing.

Sect. 5. The Vestry shall cause the return of the judges of the election to be entered at large upon their minutes; and in case of vacancies by resignation or otherwise, such vacancies shall be filled by persons chosen by the remaining Vestrymen, and who shall continue in office until the next annual election ; the result of the election shall be publicly announced in the Church on the Sunday next following.

Sect. 6. In case of a failure to elect Vestrymen on Easter Monday, then the election may be held at any other time, which the Vestry in office shall appoint for that purpose.

ARTICLE II.

Of the Meetings of Vestry, Election, Order of Business, &c.

Sect. 1. The stated meetings of the Vestry shall be held on Easter Tuesday, and thereafter on the first Tuesday in the months of June, October and January, throughout the year, at such time and place as the Vestry may appoint.

Sect. 2. Five members shall constitute a quorum for the transaction of business: *Provided*, That no sum of money exceeding one hundred dollars shall be disposed of, nor any salary increased, unless the notices of such meeting shall contain the words, " money to be disposed of," or unless eight members of the Vestry be present, the consent of a majority of whom shall be necessary.

Sect. 3. At the first stated meeting after their election. the Vestry shall, pursuant to the seventh article of the Charter, elect one of their number who shall be " The Accounting Church Warden," the Rector shall appoint another member of the Vestry who shall be " The Rector's Church

Warden." The Vestry shall then elect a Secretary, from
their own body; and shall also elect such other officers as
may be necessary. The Vestry shall also elect Lay Deputies
to represent the Parish in the Diocesan Convention, as required by the Canons of the Church. In case of failure to
elect officers and Lay Deputies, or either of them as aforesaid, the election may be held at any subsequent meeting of
the Vestry. All elections shall be by ballot, unless the same
shall be dispensed with by unanimous consent.

SECT. 4. The Rector, either Church Warden, or any two
of the Vestry, may require the Secretary to call special meetings, and written notice of any such meetings shall be left
at the house or place of business of each Vestryman at least
twenty-four hours before the proposed time of meeting, sig-
nifying the time and place and object thereof.

SECT. 5. The Rector, or in his absence the Rector's Church-
Warden, shall preside at the meetings of the Vestry; but if
both shall be absent, then any other member present may be
appointed Chairman for the time.

ARTICLE III.

Of the Election of a Rector or Assistant Minister.

SECT. 1. For the election of a Rector, or Assistant Minister, at least eight votes of the Vestry shall be necessary:
Provided, That the consent of the Rector shall always be
necessary to render the election of an Assistant Minister
valid.

SECT. 2. In either case, the person to be elected must have
been openly nominated, at a previous meeting of the Vestry,
the notices of which shall have been issued at least one week
previous to the holding thereof, and shall have expressed
therein, that such nomination would then be made and received; and the notices for the meeting, at which such election is intended, shall express such intention; and no election

as aforesaid shall be held, until at least two weeks shall have elapsed from and after the nomination of the candidate or candidates.

SECT. 3. The election of a Rector or Assistant Minister shall be by ballot.

SECT. 4. In the case of the election of a Rector or an Assistant Minister, publication thereof shall be made on the next ensuing Sunday, by the officiating minister, morning and evening.

ARTICLE IV.

Of the Church Wardens, Secretary and Sexton.

SECT. 1. The Church Wardens shall have a general superintendence over the property of the corporation, and shall take care that the Sexton and other officers perform their respective duties in a satisfactory manner, and that order be maintained in and about the Church during the time of divine service. They shall have power to make purchases of all articles necessary for the use of the Church, not exceeding in amount one hundred dollars per quarter, unless by order of the Vestry.

SECT. 2. The Accounting Church Warden shall have the custody of the title papers, seal, and account books of the Corporation. He shall have charge of all the revenues of the Corporation, which he shall deposit in one of the banks of this city, to his credit as Accounting Warden of St. Clement's Church, and shall disburse them under the orders of the Vestry, and shall enter in a book, to be kept for the purpose, all sums received and paid by him, which book shall be open to the inspection of the Vestry if required. He shall pay the Rector, and all other officers of the Corporation respectively, the stated salaries or compensation quarter-yearly. And for all payments made by him, he shall take full and proper receipts, as his vouchers therefor. He shall render to the Vestry annual accounts of all receipts and disbursements at the stated meeting on Easter Tuesday; and shall at that time have prepared and lay before the Vestry, a statement of all the debts and liabilities of the Corporation, in detail, and to whom the same are owing, respectively; and also a statement of all the property, claims, and effects belonging to the Corporation, which accounts shall be referred to a committee to be audited. He shall have special charge of the communion plate, &c., and shall provide the bread and wine necessary to the administration of the Holy Communion. It shall be the duty of the Vestry to collect the alms of the congregation when required.

Sect. 3. The Secretary shall keep regular minutes of the proceedings of the Vestry, notify its members of all its meetings, call special meetings when required, and perform generally such duties as appertain to the office.

Sect. 4. All books and papers, the property of the Corporation, shall be delivered by the Secretary and Wardens to their successors in office.

Sect. 5. The Sexton, besides his constant care of the Church, shall perform all other duties connected with its affairs which shall be required by the Rector or either of the Wardens.

ARTICLE V.

Registers.

The Accounting Church Warden shall provide a book, to be kept under lock in the Vestry room, in which the Rector or officiating Minister shall enter an account of all marriages, baptisms, confirmations, and funerals at which he shall have officiated—the record to state the date of the marriages, and names of the parties, with the names of the parents; the date of the birth of the child baptized, with its name and those of the parents and sponsors; the name of the adult baptized, with those of the sponsors; the name of the person confirmed; and the name and age of the person buried, with the date of his or her death.

This book shall belong to, and remain with the Vestry as part of the Church Records.

Certificates from these records, under seal, shall, when requested, be given without charge, by the Wardens.

ARTICLE VI.

Committees.

The Standing Committees shall be appointed by the Rector, and shall consist of three members on the Committee of Accounts, three members on the Committee on Music, five members on the Committee on Distribution of Collections, three members on the Committee on Sunday Schools, three members on the Steeple and Bells.

ARTICLE VII.

Pews and Pew Rents.

SECT. 1. Any person may acquire a right to hold permanent sittings in the Church, the Vestry not objecting, by paying such a sum as shall have been assessed upon such sittings by the Vestry, a list of which shall always hang in the Vestry room: *Provided,* That no person shall hold less than all the permanent sittings in one pew.

SECT. 2. All other sittings shall be termed "rented sittings," and shall be set forth and described in a book to be kept for that purpose. No such sitting shall be rented for any term exceeding one year from the next semi-annual collection day; and the rent or compensation shall be payable semi-annually in advance on the first Mondays of April and October. The actual renter not being in arrears, shall have a preference over any other applicant for the same sitting or sittings.

SECT. 3. A register of permanent and rented sittings in the Church shall be kept by the Accounting Church Warden.

SECT. 4. All transfers of permanent sittings shall be made in writing, in a book to be kept for that purpose by the Accounting Church Warden, but no transfer shall have any effect until it be approved by the Vestry, and entered in the said register.

SECT. 5. The Accounting Church Warden shall have power to let any vacant sittings, subject to the approbation of the Vestry, and he shall report at each meeting all the sittings let since the last meeting, which, being approved, shall be entered on the Minute Book of the Vestry.

SECT. 6. When the same pew is rented by more than one person, no particular part of the pew shall be considered as belonging exclusively to any or either of them, and in case of dispute, the Accounting Warden shall adjust the same. If either of the parties shall refuse to acquiesce, the matter shall be decided by the Vestry.

SECT. 7. If any person holding permanent sittings in the Church, shall let, sell, or otherwise dispose of the same to any other person, without the consent of the Vestry, his right therein shall be forfeited.

SECT. 8. The pew rents shall be payable in such place as the Vestry may designate semi-annually, on the first Mondays in April and October in each year; and all persons indebted for pew rent shall be bound to pay the same then and there, without further demand.

SECT. 9. If any person shall, for the space of six calendar months, be in arrear for a year's pew rent, for any sitting or sittings, the Accounting Church Warden shall have power forthwith thereafter to let the same as vacant. Or if any person holding permanent sittings in the Church, shall be in arrear for the tax upon the same for the space of two years, his or her right therein shall be forfeited.

SECT. 10. When any permanent sittings shall be forfeited, the same shall be reported to the Vestry, and being approved, the name of the holder shall be erased from the register.

SECT. 11. The tax upon permanent sittings shall be as directed from time to time by the Vestry.

SECT. 12. The carpets of the pews shall not be removed from the Church except by order of the Vestry: the cushions of the pews shall be uniform in color and material, as directed by the Vestry.

ARTICLE VIII.

Seal of the Corporation.

The Seal—representing a celestial crown with the circumscription. "Sigillum Ecclesiæ S. Clementis. Philada."—shall be of metal: it shall be used in all acts of the Vestry requiring the seal, and only by their order.

ARTICLE IX.

Repeal or alteration of the By-laws.

No repeal or alteration of these By-laws shall be made. unless proposed at a previous meeting. and adopted by two-thirds of the members present: the notices for both meetings having expressed that alterations in the By-laws will be proposed or acted upon.

Affidavit of W. H. N. Stewart.

I. I am the Assistant Minister of St. Clement's Church. Philadelphia. and entered upon the duties of my said office on or about Easter day. 1869. My salary is $500 a year.

II. I have during all of the time of my connection with said Church. received only three communications from the Vestry of said Church: the first calling me as Assistant Minister of said Church: the second conveying resolutions of thanks for a memorial window I put therein. and the third dismissing me therefrom.

III. I have never been charged. presented. or tried for any offence whatever. and I have never had any quarrel with any member of said Church, but on the contrary. have had the assurance of large numbers of them of their confidence in me, and their desire that I should not leave said Church.

IV. When I was called to and accepted the Assistant Ministership of St. Clement's Church, no terms in regard to any tenure were stipulated and agreed upon between me and the Vestry, or congregation of the said Church. There was no contract of hiring between us, for a year or any other term, but I accepted the office according to the usage of the Protestant Episcopal Church. I have always understood it to be, until the relation of Minister and people was dissolved by mutual consent, or the Minister was removed for cause shown after trial or regular investigation. I have been in the ministry of the Church twenty-seven years, and nineteen of them in the United States, and have had charge of four Parishes in that time. I have never known of the dismissal of a Minister by the *ex parte* action of any one, Vestry, or congregation, or Bishop, and I have always understood and believe, that I am not at liberty to leave the Church of my own Parish by my own mere motion, but that I must have the consent of the Parish, or obtain permission from the authorities of the Diocese for cause shown.

Affidavit of Walter H. Tilden.

I. I am a member of St. Clement's Church, and a pew-holder therein, and have been such about four years. I have been a Vestryman of said Church, and favored Mr. Walden while he was the Rector of the Church, and now favor Dr. Batterson, and Dr. Stewart; and, so far as I know the sentiments of the congregation of said Church, I believe they are by a large majority in favor of the present Ministers.

II. Some time ago, I had a conversation with Mr. Morris, concerning the Ministers of St. Clement's Church. He said to me, that as the Vestry called the Ministers, they could discharge them. I asked him what would be the consequence if they would not be discharged, when he said they could close the doors of the Church, and thereby keep them out.

He further said, that he would rather see the Church closed than kept open under the present Ministers.

III. From my knowledge of the sentiments of the pew-holders and congregation of said Church, I believe that a large number of them will leave said Church, if the acting Vestry of the Church be permitted to deprive them of the Ministers of their choice.

Affidavit of C. Gedney King.

I. A short time prior to the Easter election, I was riding in a Walnut street car, in which were seated Mr. George N. Allen and a friend, conversing together about St. Clement's Church, and the election then near at hand. Mr. Allen's friend asked him what they were going to do if they (the Vestry party) were successful at the election. Mr. Allen said, that rather than have the thing go on as it was, they would close the Church; that Dr. Batterson had thrown down the gauntlet and they would take it up.

Affidavit of Elias L. Boudinot.

I. I am a member of, communicant, and constant attendant at St. Clement's Church, and have been a pew-holder in said Church for the two years last past.

II. I desire that the connection of the Rev. Drs. Batterson and Stewart with the said Church should remain unbroken, and believe such to be the wish of a large majority of the congregation.

III. I believe that should the action of the present (*de facto*) Vestry be sustained, it would injure the financial affairs of said Church, and would depreciate the value of pew-holdings.

Affidavit of Charles B. Stewart.

1. I am a member of St. Clement's Church, and have been a constant attendant and pew-holder in said Church for

the great part of the time since the Church was formed and for the two years last past.

II. I desire the Rev. Drs. Batterson and Stewart should retain their connection with said Church, and I believe that a majority of the congregation are unwilling that they should leave it.

Affidavit of M. Morris Marple.

I. I am a pew-holder and attendant at St. Clement's Church, and have been such for the last two years, and am not a member of any other church.

II. I desire that the connection of the Rev. Drs. Batterson and Stewart with said Church should remain unbroken, and I believe that to be the desire of a large majority of the congregation of said Church.

III. I believe that if the action of the present acting Vestry be sustained, it would cause many of the members and pew-holders to leave said Church, and thereby injure the financial affairs thereof, and depreciate the value of the sittings.

Affidavit of Henry L. Marple.

I. I am a member, communicant, regular attendant, and pew-holder of St. Clement's Church.

II. I desire that the connection of the Rev. Drs. Batterson and Stewart with said Church should remain unbroken, and I believe that to be the desire of a large majority of the congregation of said Church.

III. I believe that should the action of the present Vestry be sustained, it would injure the financial affairs of said Church, and would depreciate the value of sittings therein.

Affidavit of Richardson L. Wright, Jr.

I. I am a member, communicant, pew-holder and attendant at St. Clement's Church, and favor the Rev. Drs.

Batterson and Stewart as the clergy thereof, and believe that a large majority of the communicants and pew-holders of said Parish and Church are of the same mind.

II. I believe that if the action of the acting Vestry be not restrained, large numbers of the congregation and pew-holders would leave the Church, to the great detriment thereof, financially and spiritually, and that it will deter others from connecting themselves with said Church, and thereby render it impossible to dispose of my holding for the remainder of my term, and deprive me of the value and benefit thereof.

Affidavit of John L. Kates.

I. I am a pew-holder in St. Clement's Church, Philadelphia, and have been for ten years.

II. I attend said Church frequently, as also do my family, and I do not attend any other Church than St. Clement's.

III. I favor Drs. Batterson and Stewart as the Ministers of said Church, and am opposed to the action of the Vestry in their efforts to dismiss said Ministers; and all of my family are of the same opinion in this respect.

Affidavit of Henry N. Barnes.

I. I am a member, communicant, and regular attendant at St. Clement's Church, Philadelphia, and have been a pew-holder therein for the last five years, the allegation of the defendants in their answer to the *quo warranto*, to the contrary thereof, notwithstanding.

II. I desire Drs. Batterson and Stewart to remain in the said Church, and I believe that a large majority of the actual attendants, communicants, worshippers, and pew-holders are of the same way of thinking; and that if the Acting Vestry succeed in dismissing said Ministers, a large majority of the worshippers and pew-holders will leave said Church, to the great detriment thereof, spiritually and financially.

Affidavit of Lewis G. Bull.

I. I am a member of and pew-holder in St. Clement's Church, Philadelphia, and have been such for seven years. I have regularly paid the pew rent thereof, and have the receipts therefor, some of them being issued in the name of Mr. Lewis G. Bull, and some in the name of Mrs. Lewis G. Bull. At the Easter election, 1871, I was told that the pew stood in my wife's name, when I offered to vote and was refused the right ; whereupon I brought my wife, and went with her and voted.

II. I and my wife and family favor Drs. Batterson and Stewart as the Ministers of said Church, and hope that they may be sustained in their offices.

Affidavit of Samuel Ritchie.

I am well acquainted with Joseph R. Wilkins, Jr. He is an attendant at St. Clement's Church. He has a pew therein, which he rents from the Church, and has held about one year. Before he took said pew, he rented one-half of a pew from Mrs. Thaddeus Norris, and paid the rent therefor to her.

The following affidavits were read on the part of the defendants.

Affidavit of John Lambert.

JOHN LAMBERT, being duly *affirmed*, deposes and says, that he is instructed, and believes none of the complainants are members of the Rector, Church Wardens and Vestrymen ot St. Clement's Church, in the City of Philadelphia, a body politic, as set forth in said bill. Not one of them owns, or has ever owned, a pew in the said Church, though some ot them are members of the Church, entitled to vote. The complainants, with the exception of Hermon G. Batterson

4

and W. H. N. Stewart, and Lewis G. Bull, are renters of pews and sittings in said Church. The said Hermon G. Batterson and W. H. N. Stewart do not, nor does either of them, rent a pew or sitting in said Church, and neither of them has ever paid for or held a pew or sitting in said Church. The said Lewis G. Bull is not the owner or renter of a pew or sitting in said Church, and his name does not appear on the Vestry books. Of the complainants, J. C. Morrison, J. Douglass Brown, William A. Rolin, Stephen Fuguet, M. Morris Marple, Henry N. Barnes, and Walter H. Tilden, only, were competent to vote for Vestrymen at the election held on Easter Monday, April 10th, 1871. They only of the complainants appearing by the Vestry books to have paid two successive years immediately preceding the time of said election, for a pew or sitting in said Church.

That John Lambert, Henry Henderson, Henry Norris, and Charles S. Pancoast, of the defendants, are each pew owners in said Church, and are undoubtedly members of said Corporation. That Henry C. Thompson, Henry S. Lowber, P. Pemberton Morris, George N. Allen, James Dougherty, Francis R. Abbott, Edward Borhek, and T. Franklin Cooper, of the defendants, are renters of pews or sittings in said Church, and appear by the Vestry books to have paid two successive years immediately preceding the time of said election, for a pew or sitting in said Church, as do also the said John Lambert, Henry Norris, and Charles S. Pancoast. The said defendants now exercise the office of Vestrymen, having, as they believe, been regularly and duly elected thereto on the 10th day of April, 1871, each and all of them being by the Constitution and By-laws of said Corporation duly qualified to act as such Vestrymen.

The statements of the bill as to the issuing, service, and pendency of a writ of *quo warranto* in the Supreme Court, are true.

The statements of the bill as to the election of the Rev. H. G. Batterson, and the Rev. W. H. N. Stewart, to the offices of Rector and Assistant Minister respectively, and as to the amount of salary paid them, are true.

The resolutions recited in the fourth article of the bill

were presented and passed as therein stated; and the statement in said article of the action of the Rev. H. G. Batterson and the Vestry respectively, is true.

The deponent further says that Messrs. Lambert and Morris laid said resolutions before the ecclesiastical authority of the said Diocese on the third day of May, 1871, and that the Right Rev. Wm. Bacon Stevens, Bishop of the Diocese of Pennsylvania, concurred in the same on the fourth day of May, A. D. 1871.

This deponent further says that, to the best of his knowledge and belief, the defendants are now, and were at the time of their action upon the said resolutions, the legal representatives and duly elected Vestry of said Church. That their action upon said resolutions was regular, canonical, and lawful. That with the concurrence of the ecclesiastical authority, they had full power to dissolve the connection between the Church and its Rector and Assistant Minister, and that that connection is dissolved and was dissolved before the said injunction was served, in accordance with the Constitution and Canons of the Protestant Episcopal Church in Pennsylvania, and in the United States.

That the defendants never intended, as alleged in the bill, pending their efforts to obtain for their action the concurrence of the ecclesiastical authorities, to prevent, by acts of force, the exercise by the Rector and Assistant Minister of the functions of their respective offices within St. Clement's Church.

The deponent further says that John Lambert, Henry Henderson, Henry Norris, and Charles S. Pancoast, of the defendants, the Executors of the Estate of the late Wm. Savery Wilson, Dr. J. A. McCrea, George W. Hunter, and Simon Delbert (the four last named not taking part with the complainants in these proceedings), are the only parties owning any pews in the said Church, except the Corporation itself, which is the donee of the said W. S. Wilson, of thirty-six pews. And that the said Henry Henderson owns eight, and the Estate of W. S. Wilson one hundred and thirty-seven pews. They are the only parties interested as proprietors in the Church property. There can be no damage, as this deponent believes, to the leasing value of complainants' pews, as they own none.

The deponent further says, that the complainants, Charles B. Shillitoe, Samuel Ritchie, Richardson L. Wright, Jr.. Henry N. Barnes, J. C. Morrison, John Huggard, Stephen Fuguet, Walter H. Tilden and C. Gedney King, who were renters of pews up to April 3d, 1871, have not paid the pew rent due in advance from that day, and, if renters of pews, are in arrear since said April 3d, 1871.

Additional Affidavit of John Lambert.

John Lambert further avers, that the Vestry of St. Clement's Church, for the year from Easter Monday, 1871, to Easter Monday, 1872, is composed of the following named persons, to wit: John Lambert, Henry S. Lowber, P. Pemberton Morris, Henry Henderson, Henry Norris, George N. Allen, Henry C. Thompson, James Dougherty, Charles S. Pancoast, Francis R. Abbott, Edward Borhek, and T. Franklin Cooper. And that the Vestry for said Church for the year from Easter Monday, 1870, to Easter Monday, 1871, was composed of some of the same persons, to wit: John Lambert, Henry S. Lowber, P. Pemberton Morris, Henry Henderson, Henry Norris, George N. Allen, Henry C. Thompson, James Dougherty, Charles S. Pancoast, and Francis R. Abbott, and also Walter H. Tilden and Charles B. Stewart, which last two named are now relators in the suggestion for the writ of *quo warranto*, brought before the Supreme Court against the present Vestry of said St. Clement's Church.

Deponent further says, that the encumbrances against said Church, are a ground rent of fourteen hundred (1400) dollars per annum, and bonds and mortgages amounting to ten thousand (10,000) dollars, secured on the Parish building : together with sundry indebtedness not secured by liens.

Additional Affidavit of John Lambert.

John Lambert, being duly *affirmed* according to law, doth depose and say, that he is Accounting Warden of St.

Clement's Church, in the City of Philadelphia, and as such has possession of the Vestry books.

That the following named persons are owners and renters of pews in said Church, from the dates set opposite their respective names. (Here follows a list of 96 names.)

And the deponent saith that the above statements, taken by him from the Vestry books, are true to the best of his knowledge and belief.

Mr. HANSON then addressed the Court on behalf of the plaintiffs. He said—

This case is peculiarly free from a dispute as to the facts, and so far as they affect the question now before the Court in its strictly legal character, they are these.

On the 10th April, 1871, the regular annual election for the Vestrymen of St. Clement's Church was held. The result was a declaration by the judges of election, that Mr. Lambert and others (the defendants here) were chosen to be Vestrymen from Easter Monday, 1871, to Easter Monday, 1872, and those gentlemen accordingly entered upon the performance of their duties. On the 18th April, 1871, Mr. Tilden and others, who had contested with Mr. Lambert and others, in the election to the office of Vestrymen, filed in the Supreme Court a suggestion for the writ of *quo warranto;* the writ was allowed and made returnable to the first Monday of May following. The suggestion alleged that Mr. Lambert and others were not duly and lawfully elected, and charged that votes of those who under the charter of the Church were not legal voters, were received for Mr. Lambert and those acting with him, and that the votes of others (among them the Rector and the Assistant Minister) who offered to vote for Mr. Tilden and others, and who were legally qualified voters, were rejected; and that had the first class of votes been rejected, and the second class received, Mr. Tilden and the plaintiffs in the *quo warranto* proceedings, would have been the rightfully elected Vestrymen. The proceedings in the *quo warranto* are still pending. At a meeting of the acting Vestry, held 3d May, 1871, Mr. Thompson presented to the meeting a series of resolutions, proposing with the concurrence of the

42

Ecclesiastical authority of the Diocese, to dismiss the Rector and the Assistant Minister from their offices. No reasons for this course were assigned. The Rector, who presided, declined to entertain any action upon the resolutions, on the ground that the attempted course was not within the scope of the Vestry's authority, and he refused to entertain an appeal from his decision. The acting Secretary of the meeting, at the request of one of the Vestrymen, submitted the resolutions for the action of the Vestry ; and disregarding the presence of the Rector and without his action, the resolutions were adopted. The meeting adjourned to meet on Saturday, 6th May, 1871.

On the day following that of the Vestry meeting, that is, 4th May, the Rector and others, parties plaintiff, filed their bill praying for an injunction to restrain the defendants from interfering with the exercise by the Rector and Assistant Minister of their offices in St. Clement's Church, until a canonical dissolution of the connection existing between them and the congregation shall have taken place in accordance with the canons of the Protestant Episcopal Church ; and under the new equity rules an *ex parte* injunction issued. On the same day, May 4th, a notification of this action of the Rector and others was sent to the Bishop of the Diocese.

By the affidavits filed on behalf of the present defendants, it appears that the Bishop – on the day following the Vestry meeting, and on the very day on which the injunction issued, and notice of its exit was sent to him—with a haste that counsel for defendants may show to have been well considered, concurred in the action of the Vestry ; although, neither by the Vestry nor by any one, had there been a presentment against either the Rector or Assistant Minister ; neither a hearing nor a trial.

Not only have the defendants sought to do that which they had no lawful power to do, but their action has been that of a body whose very existence the Commonwealth had called in question, seeking, in disregard of the wishes of their constituents, of the wishes of more than two-thirds of the communicants of the Church, and of those who occupy pews and sittings, as the affidavits show, to sever the connection between the Church and its Rector and Assistant Minister; and this without a cause alleged or a charge made.

The aid of equity is invoked on two grounds.

I. To protect legal rights to property from irreparable injury pending litigation. This is part of the original and proper office of a court of equity.

II. To restrain an act wholly illegal, and from which, if not restrained, irremediable damage will flow.

The legal rights alluded to, and which the Rector and Assistant Minister have, are 1. The right to their salaries. 2. The right to pursue their avocations. This is a property, an estate in their professions. In *Cummings v. State of Missouri*, 4 Wall. 277–320, in reply to the argument of counsel for the State, that to deprive one of life, liberty and property, was punishment, but to take from one a right to exercise a vocation was not, Mr. Justice Field, in showing the fallacy of this, said, "He does not include under property those " estates which one may acquire in professions, though they " are often the source of the highest endowments and honors."

The legal rights of those having sittings and rented pews, are 1. The enjoyment of the right to meet and hear the teachings for which they have paid. 2. The right to transfer their sittings for a consideration, which would be barred if the Rector is dismissed. The character of a pew-right is described in *Church v. Wells' Executors*, 12 Harris (24 Penna.), 249. 3. The right to require the body to whom is delegated the power to collect and apply funds, that such body shall apply said funds in accordance with the trust accepted. "It ap- " pears that the funds of the institution are under the con- " trol of the governing body, and the defendants have prac- " tically the power of withholding from the plaintiff the " emolument assigned to and accepted by him. This consti- " tutes a trust which they have to perform, and which they " are bound to perform in favor of the person who fills the " office of pastor, and accusing the plaintiff to be wrongfully " deposed. I am of opinion, the relation of trustee and " cestui que trust does exist, &c." *Dauguars v. Rivaz*, 28 Beavan, 233–247.

In order to obtain protection of legal rights pending litigation, the plaintiffs must show 1. That there is a real question in litigation. 2. That there will be irreparable injury. 3. That the weight of inconvenience (in balancing between interfering and not interfering) is greatly in favor of plaintiffs. In the *Great Western Railway Co.* v. *The Birmingham and Oxford Junction Co.*, 2 Phillips, 597–602, Lord Chancellor Cottenham said: " It is certain that the Court will, in many " cases, interfere and preserve property in *status quo* during the " pendency of suit in which the rights to it are to be decided, " and that without expressing and often without having the " means of forming any opinion as to such rights." * * * " In order to support an injunction for such purpose it is not " necessary for the Court to decide upon the merits in favor " of the plaintiffs. If, then, this bill states a substantial " question between the parties, the title to the injunction " may be good, although the title to the relief prayed " may ultimately fail." In *Daly* v. *Archbishop of Dublin*, Flanegan & Kelly's Rep. 263 (Rolls Court), the Master of the Rolls granted an injunction to restrain the Archbishop from collating by way of lapse to a deanery, pending a suit in the Consistorial Court respecting the presentment by the chapter. *The Mammoth Vein Coal Co.'s Appeal*, 4 P. F. Smith, 183 (54 Penna.), although not a case for an injunction, yet the principle is stated by Thompson, J. " It ought not to " be forgotten that a preliminary injunction is a restrictive " or prohibitory process designed to compel the party against " whom it is granted to maintain his *status* merely until the " matters in dispute shall, by due process of the Courts, be de- " termined; the sole foundation for such an order being, in " addition to cases of the invasion of unquestioned rights, " the prevention of irreparable mischief or injury."

Irreparable injury. This must be a grievous or material injury, and not adequately reparable by damages at law. In *Mammoth Vein Coal Co.'s Appeal*, such injury is said to be " injurious consequences which cannot be repaired under any " standard of compensation." One that cannot be readily estimated in damages. A dismissal may render exercise of the Rector's avocation doubtful and uncertain. It may break up the Church, and do an injury to those who rented sittings on the faith of Mr. Batterson's Rectorship, which cannot be estimated.

Weight of inconvenience. The leading consideration is as to the comparative mischief to the parties. If, upon the balance of inconvenience, it appears that greater damage would arise to the defendants by granting the injunction in the event of its turning out afterwards to have been wrongly granted, than to the plaintiff from withholding it, in the event of the legal right proving to be in his favor, the injunction will not be granted. If it appear that greater damage would arise to the plaintiff by withholding the injunction in the event of the legal right proving to be in his favor, than to the defendant by granting the injunction, in the event of the injunction proving afterwards to have been wrongly granted, the injunction will issue.

The litigation pending under the *quo warranto* is a challenge and warning to the defendant, and the *quo warranto* is itself a cautionary writ, and should need no injunction to aid it.

II. To restrain the wholly unlawful invasion of a right. The proof is that the Ministers are regularly settled in the Church, with a perfect right to the salaries agreed upon. The action of the Vestry is unlawful, 1. Because the meeting at which the resolutions were passed was not held in accordance with the provisions of the By-laws. 2d. Because any action of the Vestry of St. Clement's Church to dismiss a Minister is *ultra vires* and void. 3. Because the Vestry have sought to disfranchise a member of the Corporation without a charge, a summons or a hearing.

The meeting was irregular. By sect. 5 of art. 2 of the By-laws, the Rector shall, if present, preside at the meetings of the Vestry. The Vestry is composed of twelve lay members. A quorum consists of five. Thus its meetings are (when the Rector is present) composed of integral parts, clerical and lay. Each part derives its right from a different source,—the Rector, from the action of the Vestry and the Bishop; the Vestry, from election by members of the Church. The Rector is such until canonically dismissed. The Vestry

change from year to year. In *Wilson* v. *McMath*, 3 Philli-
more, 67–81 (Peculiars Court of Canterbury, 1819), it was
held, that the Rector is not a mere individual of the Vestry.
He is an integral part of the parish. Sir John Nicholl said—
" The minister is not, in consideration of law, a mere indi-
" vidual of the Vestry, as has been contended, nor is he in
" any instance so described. On the contrary, he is always
" described as the first and as an integral part of the parish.
" The form of citing a parish proves this position, namely,
" as 'the *minister*, church warden, and parishioners,' he being
" specially named. Such is the legal description of a parish
" in all formal process." In *King* v. *Miller*, 6 T. Rep. 268–278,
Lord Kenyon, Ch. J., said: "This proposition seems to be
" now clearly established; that when there is a definite
" body in a corporation, a majority of that definite body
" must not only exist at the time when any act is to be done
" by them, but a majority of that body must attend the
" assembly when such act is done." In *King* v. *Williams*,
2 Maule & Selwyn, 141, Lord Ellenborough, Ch. J., said, it
is necessary that a presiding officer, who by the charter of a
borough forms an integral part of an elective assembly,
should be present up to the time when the election is com-
pleted, and an election cannot be proceeded in during his
absence, although he should improperly absent himself. In
the *Case of St. Mary's Church*, 7 S. & R. 517–538, a religious
corporation, consisting of eight lay and three clerical members, the lay members were in favor of a change of charter,
and the clerical members were not. At the meeting for
alterations, there were present seven lay and one clerical
member. Held to be an unlawful meeting, because a majority
of the integral parts of the corporation were not present.

2. Because the action of the Vestry is *ultra vires* and
void. Although this Court will not re-judge the judgment of a
Vestry (*forum domesticum*) if it has acted within the scope of its
authority, yet the Court will always see whether such tribunals have so acted. In *King* v. *Bishop of Ely*, 2 Term Rep.
290–336, Ashhurst, J., said: " If this be the true construc-
" tion of the statute, the right of nomination was an object
" of the Bishop's visitorial power. Therefore, our opinion in

" this case does not militate against any of the cases cited
" at the bar; those cases show that the acts of a visitor,
" whether right or wrong, are not to be examined in the
" courts of law, but those are cases where he has acted within
" his jurisdiction, and they proceed upon this principle that
" he is the judge whom the founder has thought fit to ap-
" point." In *Long* v. *Bishop of Cape Town*, 1 Moore, Privy
Council Cases, (N. S.) pg. 411, pg. 461, Lord Kingsdown, said:
" When any religious or other lawful association has not
" only agreed on the terms of its union, but has also consti-
" tuted a tribunal to determine whether the rules of the as-
" sociation have been violated by any of its members or not,
" and what shall be the consequence of such violation ; the
" decision of such tribunal will be binding when it has acted
" *within the scope of its authority;* has observed such forms as
" the rules require, if any forms be prescribed, and if not,
" has proceeded in a manner consistent with the principles of
" justice.   In such cases the tribunals so constituted are
" not in any sense courts ; they derive no authority from
" the Crown ; they have no power of their own to enforce
" their sentences ; they must apply for that purpose to the
" courts established by law, and such courts will give effect
" to their decisions as they give effect to the decisions of
" arbitrators, whose jurisdiction rests entirely upon the
" agreement of the parties."   See also *In re Bishop of Natal*,
3 Moore, P. C. C. (N. S.) 115 ; *Murray* v. *Burgess*, 4 Moore,
P. C. C. (N. S.) 250.   In *Dauguars* v. *Rivaz*, 28 Beavan, 233,
Sir John Romilly inquired into the right of a governing body
to dismiss a pastor from his office in the French Protestant
Church of London, and issued an injunction to prevent their
doing it. In *Com.* v. *The German Soc.*, 3 Harris, (15 Penna.) 251,
it is said the courts will preserve private tribunals within the
line of their authority, and examine whether they have jurisdiction of what they attempt to adjudicate, (explaining *Com.*
v. *Ben. Soc.*, 8 W. & S. 247 ; and *Toram* v. *Ben. Soc.* 4 Barr,
(Pa.) 519.)   In *McGinnis* v. *Watson*, 5 Wright, (41 Pa.) and
Sutter v. *Trustees*, 6 Wright, 503, the Court examined to see
if the governing bodies of churches had exceeded their powers.
So also in *Smith* v. *Nelson*, 18 Vermont, 511, 549, 566, by Ch.

Williams: *Watson* v. *Avery*, 2 Bush, (Ky.) 332, 348. And this
Court in *Leech* v. *Board of Brokers*, 2 Brewster, 571, examined
into the power of the Philadelphia Board of Brokers to expel
a member, and prevented them from doing it in that case.
The Court, therefore, having upon it the duty to examine
if the Vestry have acted within the scope of their authority,
where exists the authority to disfranchise a member of the
Corporation? In Angel & Ames on Corp. § 432, it is said:
" The power of disfranchisement and a motion, unless it has
" been confided to a particular person or class, is to be exer-
" cised by the corporation at large, and not by the person or
" class in whom the right of appointing or admitting is
" vested." And in pleading disfranchisement, if the authority is not shown in a class, it will be construed to be in
the body at large.
In *Green* v. *The Church*, 1 Sergeant & Rawle, 254, the
return stated a member was expelled by a select number.
The court said: " It is not shown by what authority they
" proceeded to try and expel a member. This is a radical
" defect, for the power of expulsion must belong to the
" society at large, unless by the fundamental article or some
" by-law founded in these articles, it is transferred to a
" select number." And to the same effect is Judge Williams'
charge to the jury in *Gordon* v. *Williams*, case of the First
Reformed Presbyterian Congregation in the City of Philadelphia, in the Supreme Court of Pennsylvania, reported in the
Legal Gazette of Philadelphia, April 14th, 1871.
Nowhere in the Charter or By-laws does there exist authority in a Vestry to dissolve the connection; neither in the Canons of the Diocese of Pennsylvania, nor in those of the Church
in the United States. The only canon on the subject is the 4th,
Title 2 of Discipline, in the Digest of Canons in the Church,
imposing penalties. It does not give expressly the right to
any one; it contemplates two kinds of dissolution of the relation—an irregular one, and a regular and canonical one.
If the Minister be dismissed by the Parish or Church, without
concurrence, then a penalty is imposed. If the Ecclesiastical
authority concurs, then the penalty is remitted; but the act
is not made regular or canonical as between the Minister and

congregation. The Vestry is nowhere mentioned in the canon, or anywhere in the prayer book, except in parenthesis, as a substitute for the Church Wardens in the office for the institution of ministers. The canon was enacted to impose a penalty upon an act which the congregation might actually but not rightfully do; which penalty may be remitted by the Ecclesiastical authority. But the dismissal is none the less an offence; although the penalty be afterwards forgiven. It is a familiar rule of law, that a statute which imposes a penalty is intended as a prohibition of the act.

The canonical dissolution is by consent, sanctioned by the Ecclesiastical authority, or by presentment, trial and punishment under Canon 2, Title 2 of Discipline.

3. Because the vestry have sought to disfranchise the Rector, &c., without a hearing or trial.

In *Bagg's Case*, 11 Coke's Rep. 93–98, King's Bench, 13 James, 1, for a mandamus, it was resolved, " and although " they have lawful authority either by charter or prescription " to remove any one from the freedom, and that they have " just cause to remove him, yet it appears by the return that " they have proceeded against him without hearing him an- " swer to what was objected, or that he was not reasonably " warned. Such removal is void, will and shall not bind the " party *quia quicunque aliquid statuerit parte inaudita altera*, " *aequum licet statuerit haud aequus fuerit*, and such removal " is against justice and right." So in *King v. Gaskin*, 8 Term Rep. 209, A. D. 1799, a return to a mandamus to restore, was held insufficient, because it did not state that the party had been summoned to answer the charge before he was removed. Kenyon, C. J., said : " If we were to hold this " return to be sufficient, we should decide contrary to one of " the first principles of justice, *audi alteram partem* * * * " It is to be found at the head of our criminal law, that " every man ought to have an opportunity of being heard " before he is condemned, and I should tremble at the con- " sequences of giving way to this principle. I have no doubt " that Dr. Gaskin has acted, on this occasion, from the best " motives, and notwithstanding our decision, he will be per-

"fectly justified in renewing his accusation against this
"person, and in removing him from his office in a more
"formal manner if the charge be true." *Doe on Demise*
v. *Gartham*, 8 Moore's Rep. 368, was an ejectment, A. D. 1823.
The visitors of a grammar school, who had dismissed the
schoolmaster for misconduct or breach of regulations of the
deed of endowment, could not recover possession of the school
house against the schoolmaster, because they had not legally
determined the schoolmaster's interest, by first summoning
him, that he might be heard in his own defence. *Queen* v.
Smith, 3 Queen's Bench, 614, A. D. 1844, was a mandamus
to restore one to his office as clerk of the parish. The return was that the clerk had misbehaved himself and had
been drunk within the view of the vicar ; to which it was
pleaded that the clerk had not been summoned to answer a
charge against him. And the return was held bad for not
showing that the clerk had been summoned. In *Jones* v.
Wright, 47 English Common Law Rep. 262, Queen's Bench,
A. D. 1844, Lord Denman, C. J., said: "No proceeding in
" the nature of a judicial proceeding can be valid unless the
" party charged is told that he is so charged, is called on to
"answer the charge, and is warned of the consequences of
" refusing to do so." In *Commonwealth* v. *The Pennsylvania
Beneficial Institution*, 2 Sergeant & Rawle, 141, a member of
a society, being in arrears three months, under the charter,
which provided, "that should any member neglect to pay
" his arrearages for three months, he shall be expelled," was
struck off the society roll, and the court held the act was
illegal ; that there should be a charge and an opportunity of
being heard. "No man should be expelled in his absence,
without notice," said C. J. Tilghman.

The resolutions of the Vestry dismissing the Rector and
Assistant Minister, were passed at a Vestry meeting, which,
in omitting the Rector as a part of it, was constituted in
disregard of the Charter and By-laws of St. Clement's
Church. The Vestry (or as it would be called in England
the Select Vestry), have nowhere granted to them by the
Charter or the Canons of the Church, the power of dismissing
the Rector which they sought to exercise, and it does not

reside in them *vertuti officii ;* admitting solely for the purpose of argument, they had this power of disfranchisement, this *quasi* judicial power, then they have exercised it in a manner which would of itself make their acts void ; what has been done was in violation of the very conception of law and judgment, and in disregard of the plainest dictates of the English and American common law.

The wrongful act affects well defined rights of property so injuriously, that it cannot be redressed by the machinery of the courts of law ; it calls for prevention ; the injury would be irreparable in the judgment of a Chancellor ; and it is clear that greater damage would befall the plaintiffs, certainly the Rector and Assistant Minister, by withholding the injunction, than to the defendants by continuing it.

The Court is therefore asked to continue the injunction heretofore granted *ex parte.*

Mr. BIDDLE, on behalf of the defendants, said—It is to be deeply regretted that this case has come before the Court. It has been ardently desired that the difficulty would be settled by arbitration outside. The present year presents the first time within the past half century, that members of this denomination have had recourse to the civil tribunals. It has been the solace of the persons of that faith, that they have been able to keep their troubles out of courts of justice. The parties to the complaint have altogether misjudged their remedy. The Ministers can leave at any time they see proper, and the Vestry can dispense with their services at any time it is their pleasure to do so. And if they think the Ministers have been wronged, they have their remedy in a civil tribunal, to bring a suit for the recovery of their salary. They should resort to the courts of law, for their salary, not to a court of equity for an injunction. They have an adequate remedy at law. This dismission is but the severance of a connection that is without terms as to time, and it cannot be pretended that when they have an action at law, they can by injunction tie up the hands of the Vestry, and continue these disorders in the Church for another year. I recognize in the fullest sense the right of men to worship according to their consciences, but it is most extraordinary that persons becoming members of a Church, accepting its rules and formulas, should, the moment they become so associated, act contrary to those rules and formulas, and when trouble arises, as in this case, say "we are martyrs to the cause of faith." If they do not like the formulas, there is a very simple thing for them to do—let them depart in peace.

The pendency of the *quo warranto* ought not to deprive the Vestry of any of its powers ; they are the *de facto* Vestry, to perform all the duties of the office fully and not by halves. This was decided in the case of the *Trustees* v. *Hill*, 6 Cowen, page 23. In that case *de facto* officers commenced and maintained an action against a party who objected that they were *de facto* officers only. But the objection was overruled.

By the Constitution and Canons of the Church, the Vestry is the ruling body, the organ of the Church, and they elect the delegates to the Diocesan Convention. The Church acts only by the Vestry.

The affidavits of a majority of the congregation ought not to have any weight here. The question is, what is the power of the Vestry, and are they acting within the scope of their authority ? This question of dismissal was passed upon at the election for Vestrymen, and now when they are successful, an effort is made to prevent them doing the very thing they were elected to do. The proceedings by *quo warranto* were intended for delay, and this Court ought not to favor that. The writ was filed in the Supreme Court, and made returnable to May, a time when it is well known that that Court would be away from this city, and sitting in another district. An issue of fact is raised in it which cannot be tried until next winter, although the real issue is one of law.

The Vestry is a body to perform its duties fully and not by halves. They are to do everything or nothing. Who is to keep the Church in repair, if the Vestry can be tied up by an injunction, or pay interest on the incumbrances, and for the music ?

This Vestry have managed the Church from its beginning.

They are the old Vestry. They have given their means to
support it before the innovations were made.

The power to elect the Rector, includes the power to dismiss him. The Vestry elects him as will be seen by the
Charter, Art. V. and By-laws, Art. III. A power of dismissal
is given by Title II., Canon 4 of the Digest of the Canons.
The title of this canon is, "Of the dissolution of a pastoral
connection." It is always proper to resort to the title of a
statute for aid in construing it. This canon treats of the
dissolution—the severance of the relation. Dismission is as
wide as the poles from degradation, or suspension. This last
punishment is inflicted when a Minister has been tried and
convicted. But there are times when it is desired to get rid
of the Minister, to sever the relation between him and the
Parish, and yet there may be no charges to make against
him, for which he can be tried and convicted. It is for such
cases at times when the Parish wishes to dismiss the Minister, and yet may not have any charge or crime to impute to
him, that the canon was enacted. In this case the Vestry
has acted within its power, has proceeded according to the
canon, and obtained the concurrence of the Bishop—the
Ecclesiastical authority.

Dr. Batterson has stated in his affidavit, that no terms as
to the time of his engagement were stipulated between him
and the Vestry. The rule of law in cases where the parties
have not fixed upon any time for the duration of the contract between them, is that either party may dissolve it at
pleasure. This was said by the Supreme Court, in *Coffin* v.
Landis, 10 Wright, 426, and *Peacock* v. *Cummings*, same
book, page 434. Who then dissolves the relation? Either
party may do it. Here the Vestry may do it. A Parish,
Church or congregation only acts by its Vestry. The Vestry
elect the delegates to the General Convention, and if they
dismiss without the Ecclesiastical concurrence, the punishment therefor falls upon them. They are deprived of representation in the Convention.

The resolutions of dismissal were introduced and passed
regularly, notwithstanding the refusal of Dr. Batterson, to
put the question to them. Mr. Murray Hoffman in his work

on " Ecclesiastical Law in the State of New York," at page 78, says, on this subject of the Rector's right to decline to put questions to a meeting of the Vestry: " Questions have also, in my experience, arisen as to the extent of the duty of a Rector, to put questions for the decision of the Vestry. There can be no doubt of his obligation to do this, in every case of a proposition properly within the province of the Vestry to act upon. It is, on the other side, clear, that he is not bound to put questions or resolutions tending to censure or criminate himself. When acts or resolutions are proposed hostile to the Rector, as under the canon respecting a dissolution of the connection, or where a Vestry is authorized to present, the body acts of necessity as Warden and Vestrymen, not as the strict integral body."

In this case the resolutions were properly put and voted for; the dismission was carried; the Ecclesiastical authority has concurred, thereby making the dismissal complete, and the injunction ought not to continue. I ask that it be dissolved.

Mr. OLMSTED, on the same side, said—

The Rector is not a member of the Corporation, nor a member of the Vestry. The Corporation owns the Church property, and it is composed of those who own pews. The Vestry is elected by the pew-holders and renters. But the owners of pews are the only ones really interested in the Church, and of these all except one are with the Vestry. The renters of the pews who favor the clergy have no pecuniary interest in this suit; they own nothing of the Church. If the property were sold, to whom would the proceeds go? Not to a pew renter, nor a communicant, nor a member of the congregation. None of these persons, therefore, have an interest which gives them a right to an injunction. Even if they had, the Vestry as the representative body has authority to act independently of them, even against their wishes. The Supreme Court of this State in the case of *Dana v. The Bank of the United States*, 5 Watts & Sergeant, page 223, held that the directors of the Bank had power to make an assignment of its assets, notwithstanding the objection and protest of the stockholders. The same principle of law applied here would sustain the action of the Vestry as against the congregation, even if the latter had any property rights.

The Vestry, by Article V. of the Charter, is composed of twelve members of the Church, but the Rector is not a member of the Vestry. He presides at the meetings of the Vestry by courtesy, not by right. He is not an integral part of the body. In relation to the rights of the Minister and congregation, in the absence of express provisions in the canons, the civil law will govern, and the principles of law concerning employer and employé apply in all their force. The employer can discharge at any time unless there be a special contract, and the employé can leave whenever he chooses to. This is the law in this State according to the cases of *Coffin* v. *Landis*, and *Peacock* v. *Chambers*, already referred to. Any other doctrine would compel a Church to sustain a Minister when he is totally incompetent to perform his duties. He might become old, infirm, sick and unable to serve in the Church; and yet if the plaintiffs' views are correct, such Minister could not be dismissed, but must remain in and be supported by his Church. This would be a great hardship.

But there is a canon on this subject which authorizes the dismissal of Ministers. It is Canon 4, Title II., and it prescribes a way by which the Parish or Church may dismiss a Minister. All that they have to do is to get the Ecclesiastical authority to concur with them and the dismissal is complete. That has been done here. In the Office for the Institution of Ministers, in the Prayer Book, the settlement of all questions between the Minister and congregation concerning a separation is reserved to the Bishop and Presbyters. We find in all the law of the Church on the subject of the dissolution of the pastoral relation, the words Parish, Church, cure and congregation used as synonyms of each other. The power of dismissal resting in either of these, is to be exercised by its representative, the Vestry.

Finally the injunction asked for ought to be refused at this stage of the cause, because it is intended thereby to compel the Vestry to restore the Ministers to the places from which they have been dismissed. It is mandatory upon them, and a mandatory injunction will never be granted until final hearing. This was decided by the Supreme Court last winter, in the case of *Audenreid* v. *Reading Railroad Co.*, reported in the Legal Intelligencer of January 13th, 1871. The plaintiffs here ask for a preliminary injunction which would be mandatory upon the defendants, and that should be refused.

Mr. PRICE, for the complainants, in conclusion said—

Dr. Batterson and Dr. Stewart are not here of their own choice or by their own act. They are only the representatives of their order; and they owe it to that order, that a wrong like that complained of here, should not go unresented. Arbitration would have been accepted gladly by them; indeed there have been frequent efforts made by them, not only to settle, but to avert such difficulties as now beset them. If scandal is brought upon the Church it is not by them; others must bear the odium. The defendants have given the cause for a resort to the Courts, and the blame for bringing this case into Court at all lies upon them. They are the wrongdoers, and Drs. Batterson and Stewart are compelled for their own sake, and for the sake of their order, to come here for protection. They seek no revenge, no gain, nothing but protection.

It has been conceded that this Court has jurisdiction to inquire whether the proceedings for the dismissal of the Ministers have been in accordance with the canons and discipline of the Protestant Episcopal Church. It can readily be shown that the proceedings now complained of have no warrant in the law of the Church.

It is proper to inquire—are these parties, before the Court as complainants, entitled to invoke that jurisdiction for the object set forth in the bill? The affidavits show that there are here complaining of the action of the Vestry, members of the Corporation; members of the Church; holders of pews and sittings; the larger part of the congregation; and the Rector and Assistant Minister. What interest is there, of any possible importance in the case, remaining unrepresented? Fewer parties would have been sufficient for the purposes of the case; but it is no valid ground of objection that so many, and representatives of all aspects of the relation of pastor and people, have manifested their deep interest in the result of this hearing by becoming parties to it. They are proper parties complaining, and that is enough. It is not necessary to look farther than the preamble to the Charter of St. Clement's Church for them. The preamble designates for whom the incorporation was asked, and the Charter is the evidence that they obtained it. Pew-owners will be found to be of no greater importance under the Charter, than other members of the congregation who hold their pews by renting them. Both are alike members of the Corporation, and entitled to appear as such, and resist the threatened injury so far as it may affect the Corporation merely.

The true relation to be regarded now, is that of Rector and congregation; that which was established after Dr. Batterson had been elected by the Vestry and accepted their call; when he was instituted or settled as the Rector of St. Clement's. The relation sought to be dissolved by a summary dismissal of the Ministers, is an ecclesiastical one; and the aid of the Bishop has been sought, showing that the defendants so regarded it. They evidently did not consider it safe to rely upon what has been set up in the argument for the defendants here, that there is a mere civil contract for hiring, made between Dr. Batterson and the Vestry, liable to be dissolved at the pleasure of either. They would not require the assistance of the Bishop to dissolve such a compact as that. But the true relation, after Dr. Batterson had become Rector, and Dr. Stewart, Assistant Minister, was ecclesiastical, as it appears by the canons and by the Office of Institution in the Prayer Book, and therefore can be dissolved only in one of the ways provided by the ecclesiastical law of that Church. The attempt to dissolve it in some other way is a grievance to the congregation, and they are therefore proper parties to the bill of complaint.

The Rector and Assistant Minister are also parties to the record. None more deeply deplore the necessity which brings them into a civil Court than they do. But the defendants,

by their conduct, have compelled them to be here. They
have no alternative but to submit to the wrong, or appeal to
a civil Court for justice. These Presbyters ought to have
been able to go to their Bishop for protection, for a hearing
at least; but as has been said by counsel for the defendants
in the course of their argument, the Bishop has already con-
sented to what the Vestry did. The announcement is heard
with surprise and regret. The Bishop was not made a party
defendant in this case, only because it was believed that he
would not consent to such a wrong as was threatened. It
was not believed that he would condemn any one of the
Ministers in his Diocese upon *ex parte* presentment, or without a hearing; and hence the Court was not asked to enjoin
him also. It will be seen now, that these Ministers find in a
civil Court their only recourse against injustice. Their congregation, except the nineteen persons who voted for the
acting Vestry on Easter Monday last, insist that they shall
resist the unwarranted action of that Vestry. It is their
duty to the Episcopal Church, and to themselves; and it is
their duty to every brother Presbyter of that Church, that
they should resist such action, and as far as they can, prevent
its passing into a precedent, upon which similiar mischief may
be done and justified hereafter. It has been shown already,
by my colleague, that the Rector is an integral part of a
Church corporation, and that he has rights which make him
a proper party to such a suit as this. But more than that,
he is the direct object of the threatened wrong.

What is the status of the defendants who undertake to
dismiss the Rector and Assistant Minister of St. Clement's?
They are the Vestrymen *de facto* only. An officer *de facto*
of a private Corporation, as St. Clement's is, may do and
perform sundry acts that will bind the Corporation; but
it is questionable whether his powers are as ample as those of
an officer *de jure*. Lord Ellenborough, in *The King* v. *The
Corporation of Bedford Level*, 6 East, 368, defined such an
officer to be one who has the reputation of being the officer
he assumes to be, and yet is not a good officer in point of
law. If the right of a public officer, as a sheriff, or mayor
of a city, to hold his office is contested, the incumbent

may discharge all official duties, but that is upon the ground of a public necessity. It is admitted that a *de facto* officer of a private corporation, may perform acts required to preserve the corporation; he may bind the corporation to one who has paid a valuable consideration for the corporate act; he may bind the corporation to third persons, and do some other acts which shall be binding. He may sue for and recover an annual subscription to support the Church, as in the case cited from 6th Cowen. But it is denied that an officer *de facto* may so act as to impair or destroy the usefulness of the corporation. The officer whose right is entire and unquestioned, is but the agent of the body. The affidavits in this case shows that out of about ninety pew-holders, fifty-eight are opposed to the action of the Vestry : out of three hundred and one communicants of St. Clement's, two hundred and seven are also opposed; and we do not know, and have not heard of any in favor of the Vestry, other than the nineteen who voted for them. It is incumbent on those who have undertaken so serious a business as this dismissal, against the will and desire of the congregation, to show a good and sufficient warrant for it. What warrant have they shown? It has been urged upon the mercenary footing of a contract of hiring, alleged to be made between the Vestry and the Ministers, for no definite period, and therefore liable to be terminated at the will and pleasure of either party to it; and that is urged as decisive of the whole question, as though such a contract were the only bond between a Rector and his congregation in the Episcopal Church. It might be instructive to know, whether the Bishop concurred in the Vestry's resolutions of dismissal, upon such grounds. It is not probable that he did. It is more probable that he would be as much surprised to learn that the dismissal is sought to be justified in that manner, as many others were surprised to learn that he had concurred in the resolutions to bring it about. But no such thing exists, in fact, as a contract between the Vestry and the Rector of St. Clement's.

It was said also, that the Vestry of St. Clement's have, by the Charter, an implied power to dismiss the Ministers, because the Charter gives to the Vestry express power to elect them. The answer is an obvious one. The powers of election and dismissal are dissimilar; and if a special delegation of power to the Vestry was necessary to enable them to elect a Rector and Assistant, it would require an express power to enable the Vestry to dismiss them; and that power cannot be found in the Charter. There are reasons arising from the Ecclesiastical relation between a Rector and his congregation, under the laws and discipline of the Church, which would make it improper to introduce such power into a charter. An alleged cause of dismissal is, under the Ecclesiastical cognizance, and must be inquired into by a tribunal provided by the canons of the Church.

Canon 4 of 1804, respecting differences between Ministers and their congregations, not now in force, has been referred to as showing what has been the sense of the Church on this subject. It provided that in cases of controversy between rectors of churches and the Vestry or congregations of such churches which could not be settled by themselves, either party might make application to the Bishop. And if it appeared to the Bishop and his Presbyters, that the controversy had proceeded to such lengths as to preclude all hope of its favorable termination, and that a dissolution of the connection was indispensably necessary to restore the peace and promote the prosperity of the Church, the Bishop and his Presbyters were to recommend the Minister to relinquish his charge, on such condition as should appear reasonable and proper to the Bishop and his Presbyters. If the Rector refused to comply, then the Bishop and his Presbyters were to proceed according to the canons of the Church, to suspend him from the exercise of ministerial duties within that Diocese; and if the congregation or Vestry refused compliance with the recommendation of the Bishop and his Presbyters, they were to be prohibited from sitting in the Convention.

For the case of disagreement merely, there was a well-known tribunal, the Bishop and his Presbyters, a hearing of both parties, and a suitable recommendation, in advance of action under other canons. There has always been in the Episcopal Church a negation of *ex parte* proceedings, and of ˙

arbitrary power. The sense of the Church on that subject was expressed in the first Pastoral Letter of the House of Bishops in the General Convention of 1808, over the signature of Bishop White, as follows:

" From worship we proceed to discipline. And here we wish our clerical and our lay brethren to be aware, as, on the one hand of the responsibility under which we lie, so, on the other, of the caution which justice and impartiality require. The Church has made provisions for the degradation of unworthy clergymen. It is for us to suppose that there are none of that description, until the contrary is made known to us in our respective places, in the manner which the canons have prescribed. And if the contrary to what we wish, is in any instance to be found, it lies on you, our clerical and lay brethren, to present such faulty conduct, although with due regard to proof; and, above all, in a temper which shows the impelling motive to be the glory of God, and the sanctity of the reputation of his Church.

" While we are not conscious of any bias, which, under an official call, would prevent the conscientious discharge of duty, we wish to be explicit in making known to all, we think it due to God and to his Church, to avoid whatever may sanction assumed power, however desirable the end to which it may be directed. We have at least weighty reasons to restrain us from judging without inquiry, and from censuring without evidence of crime. These are ends to which men of impetuous spirits would sometimes draw. But we would rather subject ourselves to the charge of indifference, however little merited, than be the means of establishing precedents, giving to slander an advantage, against which no innocence can be a shield ; and leaving to no man a security either of interest or of reputation. Although we have no reason to complain that sentiments in contrariety to these prevail among us to any considerable extent ; yet we freely deliver our sentiments on the subject, in order to give us an opportunity of calling on all wise and good men—and we shall not call on them in vain—to aid us in resisting, wherever it may appear, that mischievous spirit which confounds right and wrong, in judging of the characters and rights of others."

The remaining point urged by the defendants is, that Canon 4, Title 2, of the General Canons, justifies a dissolution of the pastoral connection, if the Bishop concurs in making it. This brings forward the ecclesiastical aspect of the case, and presents the true point of controversy. We maintain that when a Minister has been elected to the Rectorship of a Church, and is instituted or settled as such Rector, an ecclesiastical or sacerdotal connection is established between him and his congregation, which can be dissolved only by mutual consent, or for cause duly appearing. The connection is meant to be equally permanent, in this country, whether the Rector is formally instituted or not.

The well known course of proceeding in the Church of England is the presentation of the Minister who is to fill a vacancy; and after examination, his institution by the Bishop; then the ceremony of induction into the Church and Parish in which he is to serve. When once inducted, the incumbent could be removed only for some canonical offence committed by him; and not then, until a trial and condemnation was had. The pioneers of the Episcopal Church in this country, brought a like discipline with them; and the spirit of it has pervaded the legislation and practice of that Church, and still remains. When a Minister has been elected to a Rectorship, and has accepted, and the office of institution is to be performed, the Bishop's Letter of Institution runs thus:

"And as the Lord hath ordained that they who serve at the altar should live of the things belonging to the altar, so we authorize you to claim and enjoy all the accustomed temporalities appertaining to your cure, until some urgent reason or reasons occasion a wish in you, or in the congregation committed to your charge, to bring about a separation and dissolution of all sacerdotal relation between you and them; of all which you will give us due notice; and in case of any difference between you and your congregation, as to a separation and dissolution of all sacerdotal connection between you and them, we, your Bishop, with the advice of our Presbyters, are to be the ultimate arbiter and judge."

Here is another exclusion of assumed power, and that in an office of the Church which reaches back to the Reformation, and probably beyond it; for it does not appear that the Institution Office was changed at the time of the Reformation, when other offices were changed. The desire for a separation must be founded on a "reason or reasons;" the Bishop is to be notified of it; he is to proceed therein with the advice of his Presbyters; and that tribunal is to judge of the reasons alleged. But if it be conceded that the Bishop alone is to be "the ultimate arbiter and judge," is he to judge and determine without hearing and investigation, or, what is worse, upon hearing one side only? Every man's sense of justice revolts at that idea.

As reference has been made on the other side to a canon not now in force, to show what has been the expression of the Episcopal Church regarding the tenure by which a Rector holds his place, reference may also be made to the 29th General Canon of 1808, concerning the election and institution of Ministers into Parishes or Churches. That canon concluded thus:

"But it is to be understood that this Church designs not to express any approbation of any laws or usages which make the station of a Minister dependant on anything else than his own soundness in the faith, or worthy conduct. On the contrary, the Church trusts that every regulation in contrariety to this, will be in due time reconsidered, and that there will be removed all hindrances to such reasonable discipline as appears to have belonged to the churches of the most acknowledged orthodoxy and respectability."

Again, Canon 1 of 1795, required every Bishop to visit the Churches within his Diocese at least once in three years; but no State was to elect a Bishop unless there be at least six Presbyters residing and officiating therein. By Canon 3 of 1799, it was provided that no clergyman employed by the year, or for a limited time, shall be considered as a regularly officiating and resident Minister of the Church in any State, for the purpose of electing a Bishop under the Canon of 1795.

The canons have been moulded and remoulded from time to time, by the General Conventions of the Episcopal Church, but cardinal rules of discipline have not been changed. The Office of Institution of Ministers, which asserts the relation between the Rector and his congregation, remains the same to this day, and the obligation to investigate before a sentence of dismissal is sealed, is as binding as ever before. The part of Canon 4, relied on by the defendants, is

"In case a Minister who has been regularly instituted or settled in a Parish or Church, be dismissed by such Parish or Church without the concurrence of the Episcopal authority of the Diocese, the Vestry or congregation of such Parish or Church shall have no right to a representation in the Convention of the Diocese, until they have made such satisfaction as the Convention may require; but the Minister thus dismissed shall retain his right to a seat in the Convention, subject to the approval of the Ecclesiastical authority of the Diocese."

It is wrong, then, for a congregation to dismiss their settled Minister without the concurrence of the Bishop, and if such thing is done, the congregation is to be punished for it, by a loss of representation in the Diocesan Convention. The canon does not concede that a Vestry can dismiss under any circumstances. Does the prohibition of a dismissal without the concurrence of the Bishop, necessarily imply that it may be done with his arbitrary concurrence, and without more than that?

In what case may the Bishop concur in dismissal by the Parish or Church, in order to render it effective? Surely not when it is sought without reason, or for no cause shown. The second section of the same Canon 4, refers to the case in which the Bishop intervenes, as one of "regular and canonical dissolution between a Minister and his congregation," and provides that it shall be recorded as such. By necessary implication, it would appear that the concurrence is to be given in some canonical way. This becomes even more apparent when it is considered that the canons are the source of the Bishop's authority to deal with the Ministers in his Diocese, and that he is not the custodian of any arbitrary power. Whatever may come of the assumed power, which the House of Bishops rebuked in their Pastoral Letter, is evil. A concurrence not founded upon some canon, would be unauthorized, and therefore a concurrence to no purpose.

Again, this matter of dismissal is in the nature of a sentence and penalty. It involves the salary of the Minister, which is his right and his property, and it involves his reputation also, both of which are objects of legal protection. It appears by the affidavits read, that the sentence and penalty now threatened to be imposed, have been made up and resolved upon without accusation of the Ministers of St. Clement's, without notice to them, or hearing; and, so far as anything appears in this case, without any assigned reason or cause. In this manner the injury to reputation is to come, for no Minister can be thus summarily dismissed, without serious detriment to his reputation. Now it is argued upon the other side, that all this may be done, and that the fourth General Canon authorizes it. The complainants deny that the canon, fairly interpreted as one of a body of canons for the government of the Church, does authorize such a course of procedure, nevertheless if such be its true intent and meaning, then the canon is in conflict with the law of the land, and must fall before it.

The construction to be given to it, should harmonize it with the rest of the canons, and with the known discipline of the Church. It should not be regarded as purposely in conflict with general principles of action, which have run through all prior legislation of the Church on that subject, if it be possible to escape such view of it. That is possible, if the Bishop's concurrence is given or withheld with due regard to the provisions of other canons; and with due regard to what is contained in the Office of Institution, which is above the canons. Is this case one of difference only, between the Ministers and their congregation? Then let it be judged by the Bishop and his council, whether the council be composed of his Presbyters or the Standing Committee of the Diocese. Is the case founded upon some accusing complaint presented by the Vestry to the Bishop? Ample provision is made for that also. If it be an accusation of crime or immorality; or of holding and teaching publicly or privately, any doctrine contrary to that held by the Protestant Episcopal Church in the United States; or of violation of the Constitution or Canons of the Church; or of

any act which involves a breach of ordination vows; then
the General Canon 2, under Title 2, points out that the
Minister is to be presented and tried for either of those
offences; and if found guilty, (not otherwise,) he shall be
admonished, suspended, or degraded, according to the Canons
of the Diocese in which the trial takes place. Almost every
supposable case of sufficient importance to justify official
action, is thus specifically provided for in one way or
another. There is no need to delve into the ambiguous
language of the fourth Canon for an implied authority, to
put a sentence and punishment in advance of investigation
or trial, and thus reverse the orderly course of proceedings
for which the canons have amply provided. Such a method
of proceeding savors too much of looking up an excuse for
assumption of power, which the Church abhors.

See with what order and fairness accusations are to be
proceeded with, under the first Canon of the Episcopal
Church in the Diocese of Pennsylvania. The presentment
shall be in writing, specifying with clearness and certainty,
as to time, place and circumstance, the offence charged. It
must be made to the Bishop by the Convention, or by the
Warden or Vestry of the Parish to which the accused
belongs, or by three Presbyters of the Diocese; but the
accusers must pledge themselves to make good the accusation; and furnish in writing, the names of the witnesses and
the purport of their evidence. Then the Bishop shall cause
a copy of the presentment to be served upon the accused,
and he shall be summoned to show cause at a certain day
and place, why a commissary should not be appointed to
take and report the testimony on both sides; but either
before or after the appointment of a commissary, or after a
report by him, the Bishop shall have power to dismiss the
presentment, and declare the accused party discharged, if
the accusation contained in it appears to him an insufficient
cause of presentment in itself, or to be clearly unsupported
by the evidence. The accused shall have fifteen days' notice
of the proceeding before the commissary, who is to examine
the witnesses on both sides and take their testimony in
writing. Such is the course of preliminary examination,

with a view to ascertain whether the accusation shall be dismissed, or submitted to a Court of Presbyters for formal trial; and it is only after that formal trial and conviction that the Bishop is at liberty, under the fifth of the State Canons, to admonish, to suspend a Minister, or to degrade him from the ministry, according to the character and circumstances of his offence. But it is said on the other side, that the dismissal of a Minister is neither admonition, nor suspension, nor degradation. It is worse than the first, but not so bad as the last, which is the penalty in extreme cases only. Still it is a penalty, and more damaging to the reputation of a clergyman than admonition would be; and there must be canonical authority to warrant the infliction of a penalty of any degree. The canonical authority should be found in something better than an implication sought to be derived from ambiguous language of a prohibitory canon, which is not ambiguous however, in relation to the thing prohibited, and to which the provisions of the canon should be confined.

The defendants have not been able to produce a case, or any writer upon the law of the Episcopal Church, coinciding with their view. On the contrary, the complainants, have furnished the views of such authorities as Bishop White, Hoffman, and Dr. Hawks, who do not sustain the alleged right of a Bishop and Vestry to dismiss a Rector summarily. But if it be a fair construction of the fourth General Canon, that a Rector shall not be dismissed without the concurrence of the Bishop, therefore he may be dismissed with such concurrence; still it is insisted that the Bishop's concurrence is not to be yielded arbitrarily, but only upon proper cause shown in some orderly manner, in which both sides shall be heard and opportunity for explanation given, and then only if the circumstances of the case are found to warrant the dismissal. It must not be forgotten that Presbyters of the Episcopal Church have rights under the canons of their Church, and that they have civil rights also, and that both must be regarded. But we are asked what is to be done when a Minister becomes unable, or refuses without good cause to perform his duties and neglects them. Canon 12 of

Title 1, § vi. [3] then comes into force. By it the Bishop or
a Standing Committee, or other duly authorized persons, shall
have power to inquire into the matter, and may open the
doors of the Church to some other Minister. But by para-
graph [4] of this same canon, this shall not affect any legal
rights of property of any Parish; that is the Minister's
rights when he has become feeble and unable to serve. He
has his rights as well as the Parish, and they will always as
they have heretofore, accommodate them to each other.

The opinion of the Court was delivered May 27th, 1871, by
Ludlow, J. We approach the consideration of this case
with an oppressive sense of the responsibility cast upon us.
We see in it questions of real difficulty, involving the consideration not only of the civil law, but of the canon law of
a body of influential and respected Christians; and a question
also arises, upon the proper legal solution of which depends
the dearest rights of every Presbyter of "The Protestant
Episcopal Church" in this Diocese, and probably in this
country. We shall endeavor to solve these questions. We
mean, if possible, to be right in our conclusions; if we should
fall into error, it is a satisfaction to know that it may be
corrected elsewhere.

The case presented is simply this. An incorporated body
exists in this country known as "The Rector, Church Wardens and Vestrymen of St. Clement's Church, in the City of
Philadelphia." By the 5th Article of the Constitution,
"the election of the Vestry shall be made every year on
Easter Monday." An election took place this year according to the Charter, at the time therein specified.

On the 18th of April, 1871, a suggestion for a writ of *quo
warranto* was filed in the Supreme Court of the State. That
writ was allowed by one of the justices of that Court; and it
is now pending and is undetermined. The object of this writ
was to test the legality of the election of the defendants in
this bill, as the Vestrymen of St. Clement's Church. On the
3d day of May, 1871, a meeting of certain persons, claiming
to be the Vestry of the Church, was held, whereupon resolutions were adopted dismissing the Rector and Assistant Min-

ister (with the concurrence of the ecclesiastical authority of the Diocese) from their offices. In the affidavit of one of the defendants, it appears that on the fourth day of May, 1871, "the Right Rev. William Bacon Stevens, Bishop of the Diocese of Pennsylvania, concurred in the same." The letter or order of concurrence has not been submitted to the Court, and it is not pretended that the Rector or his assistants ever had notice from the Bishop of the matter submitted to him, or ever had a hearing or trial, or opportunity for explanation.

The contract between the Vestry and the Rector and his Assistant contained no special terms as to the tenure of office. It is admitted by the affidavits filed on behalf of the defendants, that of the plaintiffs, all except three, to wit, the Rector, his Assistant, and Mr. Lewis G. Bull, are renters of pews and sittings in said Church. It is denied that they (the plaintiffs) or either of them, own or have ever owned a pew, though some are members of the Church, entitled to vote. We are asked to give relief in three forms.

1st. To adjudge and decree that plaintiffs are members of the Corporation, etc.

2d. To restrain the defendants from dissolving the connection between the Rector and his Assistant and the congretion, and from intermeddling or taking any action therein as a Vestry or Vestrymen.

3d. To restrain the defendants, their agents or servants, from interfering in any way with the Rector and his Assistant in the exercise of their respective offices until a regular and canonical dissolution takes place.

This brief statement of the facts of the case (about which there seems to be no dispute) presents for our consideration three important questions of law, in disposing of which we think we shall be able to embrace all points presented, and thus decide this cause.

1st. Has a civil tribunal, and especially a Court of Equity, jurisdiction, and if so, are these proper parties before the Court?

2d. Can a Vestry de facto act, supposing such action to be in other respects canonical?

3d. Can a Rector, without his consent, be dismissed under

6

and by virtue of the Charter and By-laws of this Corporation, or by virtue of the canonical laws of the Protestant Episcopal Church in the Diocese of Pennsylvania, or of the Protestant Episcopal Church of the United States?

The first proposition can easily be maintained. It has been frequently decided that the civil tribunals will interfere in matters connected with disputes or contests arising out of things ecclesiastical, only, however, in so far as it is necessary to ascertain if the governing body has exceeded its power, or, in other words, has acted within the scope of its authority. The learned counsel upon both sides of this cause, during the argument, admitted this proposition, and in Pennsylvania our recent cases, *McGinnis* v. *Watson*, 5 Wright, 9, and *Sutter* v. *Trustees*, 6 Wright, 503, were decided upon principles which preclude any further discussion of the subject.

If a civil tribunal can thus take jurisdiction, a Court of Equity, under the facts of this case, and with the parties now before the Court, ought certainly to do so. While it is quite clear that we look only at the civil nature of the contract entered into between the Rector and the congregation, in a case involving a direct breach of contract, it is also certain that the very contract between the parties may give birth to rights, which, being violated, can only be maintained in a Court of Equity. The general principle contended for by the counsel for defendants, to wit, that where in an agreement for service no time is fixed, either party may dissolve the contract, (see *Coffin* v. *Landis*, 10 Wright, 426; *Kirk* v. *Hartman*, 13 P. F. Smith, p. 97,) is not denied, nor do we doubt the right of a Rector to bring an action at law for damages, against those who prevent him from entering the church building. That doctrine was clearly maintained by the Supreme Court of New Jersey, in a learned opinion delivered in *Lynd* v. *Menzies*, by Beasley, C. J., to be found reported in the American Law Register, (new series,) Vol. viii., p. 94. All we now decide is, that with the facts before us, a suit at law would be useless, and that the plaintiffs would be remediless.

Under and by virtue of the canon laws of the Protestant

Episcopal Church in the United States, a Rector, and such of his parishioners as are members of the Church, and have rented pews and sittings, who have made profession of its faith, and submitted to its government, have rights which are to be respected, (see *Conmyer* v. *United German Church*, 2 Sandf. Ch. 186,) and which, being violated, cannot be maintained by an action for damages merely. The Rector has not only a claim for the salary, which by a contract is to be paid to him, but he has also, under the charter of incorporation, those rights guaranteed by canonical law, which the petitioners desired to obtain when they " associated for the purpose of worshipping Almighty God, according to the faith and discipline of the Protestant Episcopal Church in the United States of America." The Charter being granted, the Rector and his parishioners, together with the Vestry, held rights under and by virtue of that fundamental law, which in terms " adopts the constitution, canons, doctrine, discipline, and worship of the Protestant Episcopal Church" in this Diocese, and in the United States, and acknowledges their authority.

Mutual rights and obligations were thereupon created, as sacred as any known to Courts of Equity. If these rights cannot be maintained in this Court, remediless injury may be inflicted upon the plaintiffs in this bill.

I care not now to discuss the exact legal bearing of the Office of Institution. It is enough for my present purpose to know, that when, as by the rubric directed, the senior Warden, (or the member of the Vestry,) delivered the keys of the Church to the new incumbent, he said, " In the name and on behalf of ——— Parish, I do receive and acknowledge you, the Rev. A. B., as Priest and Rector (or Assistant) of the same."

By Article 8 of the Constitution of the Church, among other things, the " Administration of the Sacraments and other Rites and Ceremonies of the Church," established by the General Conventions, shall be used in the Protestant Episcopal Churches. By virtue of the civil contract and the canon of the Church, a person becomes canonically the Rector. It is true he may or may not receive a salary ; he may or may not be an integral part of the corporation ; by the canonical law he has the right, as Rector of a certain Parish, to perform ecclesiastical duties there in that place, to wit, the Church building ; there he has the right to administer the sacraments ; there to solemnize the marriage service ; there to perform the duties incident to the public worship of Almighty God.

More than this, among other rights, a canonically settled Rector has a right to prohibit another Minister of the Church from officiating in his Parish, or within his parochial cure, without his consent. Title 1, Canon 12, sect. 6 [1] of Digest of the Canons. I quite concur with Chief Justice Beasley in the remark made by him in the case heretofore cited, when he said, " No matter in whom the title may reside, if the congregation has the use of the building, the Rector must, of necessity. have the right to partake in such use ;" and I may add, not only that he may have possession of the building, but that he may of right perform his duties there, in that place, and not elsewhere, unless at his own option. If these are the rights of the Rector, any parishioner who is a renter of a pew and constant attendant at the Church, who in good faith believes the doctrines of the Church, and submits to its government, has the equitable right to the services of the Rector of this Church within this particular Parish or parochial cure, until such services are dispensed with by competent authority.

To argue that because a civil contract exists for the payment of money, therefore, in case of a dispute, the Rector is turned over exclusively to a court of law for damages, is to run counter to the whole policy of the law ; to permit, under color of a contract, a breach, or possible breach, of rights of the most solemn character ; to confound things sacred and profane ; and this Court would be obliged to witness the utter destruction of the dearest rights, under the charter and canons of the Church, of the Rector and parishioners without power to afford equitable relief.

I will not so administer the law. I will, as a chancellor, take jurisdiction in equity; and having the parties and the cause within my judicial grasp, will treat the argument in favor of a mere action at law, and against the remedy in equity, as of the earth, earthy—it must therefore perish.

Having disposed of our first proposition, we proceed to consider the second.

Can a Vestry *de facto* act, supposing such action to be in other respects canonical?

We speak of a Vestry *de facto*, because it is not denied that by a writ of *quo warranto* the defendants' title to their office has been and is contested, and that the suit is now pending and is undetermined. "An officer *de facto* is one who has the reputation of being the officer he assumes to be, and yet is not a good officer in point of law." *Parker* v. *Keib*, 1 Lord Raymond, 658 ; *King* v. *Corporation of Bedford*, 6 East, 368. Or he is one who actually performs the duties of an office with apparent right, and under claim and color of an appointment or election. He is not an officer *de jure*, because not in all respects qualified, nor an *usurper*, who presumes to act officially without just pretence of right. *Brown* v. *Lunt*, 37 Maine, 429. We need not multiply authorities, (as was said in my opinion in *Thompson* v. *Ewing*, 1 Brewster, 121,) when the whole subject was most ably discussed and determined in *The People* v. *Cook*, 14 Barbour, before the Supreme Court of New York, and on appeal affirmed by the Court of Errors and Appeals. See 4 Selden, 67.

We do not now express an opinion as to the legality of the election held on Easter day. These defendants may be the Vestry *de jure*; but for the present, and for the purposes of this case, I am of the opinion that the Vestry is a Vestry not *de jure* but *de facto*; and by all the analogies an officer *de facto* may, without doubt, legally act in and about the duties of his office. Indeed, in one case reported it is said, where an abbot or parson, erroneously inducted, made a deed or obligation, though afterwards deprived of his benefice, yet this shall bind ; but the deed of one who usurps, before installation or induction, or who occupies in time of vacation, without election or presentation, is void. Vin. Abr. Officer and Offices, G. 3, vol. 1.

In *Baird* v. *Bank of Washington*, 11 Sergeant & Rawle, 411, the Court thought that the *de facto* title of an officer depended, not upon the question whether the appointment was void or only voidable, but whether the officer has come in under color of right or in open contempt of all right whatever; and it was further said in that cause, that the law applied not only to public, but also to private officers. Indeed, an examination of the cases upon this point, clearly satisfies me that as to third persons having an interest therein, the acts of *de facto* officers are valid; though the case cannot be found, where the right has been successfully claimed by an officer *de facto*, claiming for an act done by himself. *Riddle* v. *Co. of Bedford*, 7 Sergeant & Rawle, 392.

The case cited by the defendants' counsel, *Trustees of The Vernon Society* v. *Hill*, 6 Cowen, 23, sustains the view they take of it; and on the whole, I am inclined to the opinion (though for reasons hereafter to be stated it is not necessary to decide positively the point), that the Vestry, if otherwise competent, had authority to act.

We are thus brought to the consideration of the last point to be discussed, and which is not only the most important, but the most difficult one to decide in this case.

Can a Rector be dismissed without his consent by virtue of the Charter and By-laws of St. Clement's Church, or by virtue of any canonical law or laws whatever, of binding force, in the Protestant Episcopal Church in the United States, or in the Diocese of Pennsylvania, at this time?

We confine our investigation rigidly to the sources of power above enumerated, because we have no right to go beyond them. If the resolutions of dismissal are to be considered legal, they must be so, because sanctioned by the civil or canonical laws specified. All else is *ultra vires*, and beyond the scope of legitimate authority.

Looking now to the Charter and By-laws of the Church, I find a power vested in the Vestry to elect a Rector. See Charter, Art. 5; By-Laws, Art. 3. But upon the question of his dismissal the Charter and By-laws are silent.

By the common law, as long ago as Baggs' Case, decided in 13th Jas. 1, and reported in the 11th Coke, 99, (a,) it was determined that the power of amotion did not pass by a grant of the power to elect, as incidental to it, but must be expressly reposed in the select body by the Charter. It was assumed by Lord Mansfield, that it may be transferred to a select body by a by-law, in the same manner as the right of election. Wilcock on Corp. 247, note to sec. 634. Even if the Vestry, under *Rex* v. *Doncaster*, 1 Barnardiston, 265, had the right to make a by-law upon the subject, none now exists; and Wilcock very justly observes, that in a corporation, by charter, surely such a power must be shown to have been expressly granted by a charter or a subsequent by-law. If there is no special provision on the subject in the charter, the power of removal of a member resides in the whole body. 2 Kent, 359; *King* v. *Mayor & Burgesses of Lyne*, 1 Douglass, 149. And this last case also decides, that if special power be delegated to a part of the body, it must be shown to exist.

We think that beyond a doubt, the resolutions adopted by the Vestry are *per se* null and void, as being beyond the powers delegated by the Charter and By-laws.

Here we might pause, and for the purposes of this case, found our final order upon the view we take of the power of the Vestry, without deciding how far a congregation, with the consent of the Bishop, may dissolve the connection ; but as it is stated that the resolutions have received the concurrence of the Ecclesiastical authority of the Diocese, I will go one step further, because the question has been argued, and inquire whether on that account they are valid? If so, it must be because of some canon of the Protestant Episcopal Church in the United States, or of this Diocese, or the power which will give validity to this action of the Vestry, must be contained in the constitution of the Church itself. I have examined the canons of the Church of England for light upon this subject, not because I believe they are of binding effect here, but because as Chief Justice Beasley remarked, " the English Ecclesiastical law, although somewhat modified by new circumstances, and by American usages and statutes, constitutes the substantial basis of the law controlling the affairs of this particular Church."

These canons, by reason of the peculiar nature of the laws of England upon the subject, give us no assistance, except it may be said that no case has been discovered wherein any priest has been condemned without a hearing. The constitution of the Church in the United States, after much discussion, extending over a long period of time, from October, 1784, to August, 1789, was at this last date finally consummated and became the great Charter of the Church, the universal rule of action, and the bond of a common faith. (Hawks' Eccl. Contributions, 12.) No express power, such as is claimed in this case, is granted in terms in the constitution. If it exists at all, it must be found in the canons of the Church at large or of this Diocese.

The canons of the Diocese of Pennsylvania have been examined, and are now before me, but these are silent upon the subject; so that the only canon now in existence will be found under Title II., Canon 4, § 1, entitled "Of the dissolution of a pastoral connection." The first section declares, " In case a Minister who has been regularly instituted or settled in a Parish or Church, be dismissed by such Parish or Church, without the concurrence of the Ecclesiastical authority of the Diocese, the Vestry * * * shall have no right of representation in the convention of the Diocese, until they have made such satisfaction as the convention may require ; but the minister shall retain his right to a seat in the convention, subject to the approval of the Ecclesiastical authority of the Diocese."

" And no minister shall leave his congregation against their will, without the concurrence of the Ecclesiastical authority aforesaid ; and if he shall leave his congregation against their will, without such concurrence, he shall not be allowed to take his seat in any convention of this church, or be eligible into any church or parish until he shall have made such satisfaction, as the Ecclesiastical authority of the Diocese shall require."

The second section of this canon provides that a record shall be made of a regular and canonical dissolution, and that a dissolution not regular or canonical, shall be submitted to the Convention of the Diocese.

" This canon shall not be obligatory in those Dioceses with whose canons, laws, or charters, it may interfere."

" It will be observed," says Dr. Hawks, in his work heretofore cited, page 307, that " this canon applies to nothing but the single case of a desire for separation, which may exist without any other disagreement between the parties."

It may be further declared that no provision is made for the case of a Minister who refuses to consent to a dissolution. If a Parish or Church act without Ecclesiastical sanction, or if the Minister shall leave without the same, a penalty follows and may be inflicted; but what is to be done with a church law which, in a case like the present, prescribes no duty to be performed, creates no offence, and affixes no penalty.

I find under Title II., Canon 2, § 1, of Discipline, a series of punishable offences. For these a Presbyter may be tried, and, on being found guilty, " may be admonished, suspended, or degraded."

Is the refusal to consent to a dissolution an offence within the meaning of this canon? If so, the minister must be canonically tried. Any other doctrine would expose any Presbyter to a virtual suspension or degradation, when and as the officials of the Church, ecclesiastical and lay, might determine to strike the blow, and yet lacked either the courage or the evidence, or both, to make and sustain a direct charge or accusation.

The remarks are not intended to apply to these defendants, nor to the present most able, eloquent, and worthy incumbent of the Episcopal chair; they are intended, however, to test the true meaning of this canon and its legal effect.

If we try the proceedings of the Vestry by another standard, we will find their action altogether untenable.

Under and by virtue of a canon in force in this Diocese, a Presbyter may be tried for certain offences. This canon was doubtless adopted under the authority of the canon already referred to. See Tit. I., Canon 2, of Discipline.

Can it be possible that any Minister may be summarily ejected from his Parish without a trial?

Shall the civil law guarantee to the humblest citizen a

hearing, and may an ordained and duly instituted Minister of the Protestant Episcopal Church be denied a right as common as this one?

The Standing Committee of the Diocese of New York did not so think when in June, 1848, they acted upon a case of this description, after a copy of the written application then made, with the facts and reasons upon which it was grounded, had been served upon the Minister.

The Convention of the Diocese of New Jersey, as far back as June 6th, 1804, did not think so, when they suspended action until a canon (now repealed) was passed to meet Dr. Ogden's case. See Hoffman's Law of the Church, p. 323. That venerable prelate, whose name and opinions to this day, even in a civil Court, carry with them great weight—I mean Bishop White—did not so believe, when in speaking of the canon enacted to meet the above case, he questioned its principle on the ground that there should be no severance from a pastoral charge except as the result of a trial for alleged misconduct. Memoirs of the Church, p. 191, supposed to have been written in 1820.

In the "Office of Institution of Ministers" I find in the form of the "Letter of Institution," which a Bishop may be the rubric, send by one of his Presbyters, whom he may appoint as the institutor, the following significant sentence: "And in case of any difference between you and your congregation, as to a separation and dissolution of all sacerdotal connection between you and them, we, your Bishop, with the advice of our Presbyters, are to be the ultimate arbiter and judge." How, unless by a hearing and trial? At law and in equity, from Baggs' Case to the present day, no man or men can be condemned against his or their consent without a hearing.

But we must go one step further and endeavor to prove that without a special agreement, or in the absence of a provision in a Church Charter, or the By-laws adopted by virtue thereof, the tenure by which a Presbyter in the Protestant Episcopal Church holds his Rectorship, is by no means uncertain.

Special provisions in a Charter, or special agreements between the Rector and his congregation, become the law of the case. In England the tie cannot be broken except by judicial sentence, or resignation to and acceptance by the ordinary. Burns' Eccl. Law, Vol. III., p. 540.

In the United States, conflicting opinions exist among those best able to form a judgment upon the subject.

I am, however, of the opinion, that under the existing laws of the Church, the civil contract (except as hereinbefore specified) cannot be broken without an accusation and trial.

This opinion is based in part upon the past legislation of the Church; upon the expressed views of more than one of its oldest divines; upon the opinions of men learned in the law, who have examined the subject; upon the attempts which have from time to time been made to remedy the difficulty; and upon those general principles, which must, in the absence of express authority, govern the case. In 1804 a canon was adopted entitled "Of Differences between Ministers and their Congregations." A canon on the subject was passed, being 32d of 1808, with an additional clause. This clause was omitted in 1832. Canon XXXIV. of General Convention of 1832. This canon provides a method of trial and a penalty. In 1847, the Committee on Canons proposed a new canon, not I believe adopted, in which a system of arbitration was created. The original canon was, in 1859, repealed by the General Convention in session at Richmond, Va., on motion of the Rev. Dr. Stevens, then a Presbyter and now the Bishop of this Diocese. See Journal of Convention of 1859, pages 125–127. An unsuccessful effort was made at this Convention to amend the old canon. See Journal of Convention, p. 88, for report of Committee on Canons, by Mr. Hoffman.

The subject in 1865 was brought before the Convention of Ohio by the Bishop, and that prelate, in an address, notices as a sound principle that, "where the rights and interests of both Ministers and congregation are concerned, the body to judge should be composed of clergy and laity."

Bishop White's opinion has already been referred to, while the effort of Mr. Hoffman in the General Convention, and the expressed opinion of the late G. M. Wharton, Esq., (a

canonical lawyer of acknowledged ability,) upon the case
which arose in Michigan, (see Hoffman's Eccl. Law, p. 270.)
as well as the reported views in the last cited volume, of an
eminent Presbyter of this Diocese, Rev. M. A. De Wolfe
Howe, (whose letter, I regret to say, I have been unable to
find,) all look in the same direction.

The legislation now repealed embodied the views of the
Church upon the subject; the efforts made to amend and to
repeal the existing law both indicated a desire either to
perfect the method of trial, or to abolish it, and thus make a
Minister amenable only to canonical discipline; the expressed
opinions of prelates, presl yters, and conventions, together
with the views of prominent laymen, all seem to take it for
granted that in some method a trial should take place, and,
in default thereof, the ministerial bond should not be severed.

Upon general principles, the views already expressed in
this opinion upon other points, cover the proposition now
contended for, while the canon which declares that "a Minister is settled, for all purposes, here or elsewhere mentioned
in these canons, who has been engaged permanently by any
Parish, according to the rules of said Diocese, or for any term
not less than one year," (Tit. I., Canon 13, § 2, of Digest of
Canons,) would seem to indicate the sense of the Church to
be: *First*, That a settlement should not exist for a shorter
term than one year; and, *Second*, That unless some special
agreement, or the terms of a Charter or By-laws prohibit, it
may be indefinite.

Having thus considered the facts and law of the case, it
becomes my duty to act according to the dictates of my
judgment and conscience.

It is very evident that the interests of this Corporation are
endangered by internal difficulties of which I cannot speak,
because I have no judicial knowledge of their nature. Be
the causes what they may, it is certain that a house divided
against itself cannot stand. I therefore officially recommend
some amicable adjustment of existing difficulties. Should
an intimation to that effect be made, I will at once modify
or suspend the operation of the order about to be recorded.

The usefulness of the Rector and his Assistant will be

greatly promoted, and the peace of Vestry and parishioners re-established should the course suggested be adopted; and this is not an expression of individual opinion (which can have no place here), but of a judge clothed with the powers of a chancellor, about to exercise a most delicate prerogative; not, indeed, thereby to encourage insubordination, or wilful disregard of Ecclesiastical authority, canonically invoked, but only to prevent remediless injury.

The first prayer for relief cannot be granted at this stage of the cause; nor will I grant the second prayer in the bill contained, because the injunction would be mandatory.

The plaintiffs are, however, entitled to relief as prayed for in the third prayer of the bill; and it is therefore ordered, adjudged, and decreed that the preliminary injunction heretofore granted be continued until the further order of this Court, and that the defendants, their agents and servants be restrained from interfering in any way with the exercise by the Rev. H. G. Batterson, of his office of Rector, and with the exercise by the Rev. W. H. N. Stewart, of his office of Assistant Minister, in St. Clement's Church in Philadelphia, until a regular and canonical dissolution of the connection now existing between them and the congregation of said Church, shall take place in accordance with the Constitution and Canons of the Protestant Episcopal Church in Pennsylvania, and in the United States.

82

The following is a copy of Bishop Stevens' letter of concurrence.

DIOCESE OF PENNSYLVANIA,
EPISCOPAL ROOMS,
708 Walnut Street,
PHILADELPHIA, *May* 4, 1871.

HENRY S. LOWBER, ESQ.,
Sec'y Vestry of St. Clement's Church, Philadelphia.

DEAR SIR:—In reply to your official note of the 3d inst., enclosing certain resolutions of the Vestry, I beg leave to say that the Ecclesiastical authority of the Diocese concurs with the action taken by the Vestry in dissolving the pastoral connection between it and the Minister and Assistant Minister of St. Clement's Church.

Very respectfully yours,
WM. BACON STEVENS,
Bishop of the P. E. Church,
Diocese of Penna.

APPENDIX I.

Supreme Court of New Jersey.

WILLIAM J. LYND v. GEORGE MENZIES, JOHN H. SUYDAM, AND OTHERS.

This was an action on the case for forcibly preventing a Minister from preaching in the Church and occupying the parochial school-house. Upon the trial the following facts were elicited. By a deed dated 1st October, 1853, Cyrus Peck and wife conveyed the lot upon which the church and school-house are now erected, to the Rectors, Wardens, and Vestrymen of the Church of St. Barnabas, Roseville, in the city of Newark, in fee, upon the condition that a church and school-house should be erected thereon, and which church edifice should be consecrated, appropriated, and devoted forever exclusively to the service of Almighty God, according to the doctrine, discipline, and worship of the Protestant Episcopal Church in the United States of America. At the time of this conveyance the said Church was not incorporated, and did not become so until after the expulsion of the minister, as herein after stated.

On the 23d July, 1855, this church was consecrated by the Bishop of the Diocese of New Jersey, and from that time forward the congregation continued its organization. In December, 1861, the plaintiff accepted a call to the Rectorship of this church, and in the month of June, 1862, was duly instituted. It appeared that the plaintiff, in common with the other officers of the Church, supposed the Church had been incorporated and that various corporate acts were performed. Before his call, the Church had claimed and been conceded ecclesiastical rights which pertained to incorporated churches only; after the call of the plaintiff, a school-house was put up on the church lot, and he was placed in possession. On the 27th April, 1867, the plaintiff received a note from two of the defendants, who were the Wardens of the Church, notifying him that on Easter Day, which was then passed, his connection as Rector with the church had ceased. On the next day, which was Sunday, when the plaintiff went to the Church to officiate he found the Church closed, the doors being fastened, so as to prevent his entering. In a few days afterwards he was in a similiar manner excluded from the school-house. It was proved that such expulsions were the acts of the defendants, two of whom were Wardens and the others Vestrymen of the Church. The question of law as to the right of the plaintiff to recover was reserved, and the matter of damages submitted to the jury, who returned a verdict for $1,000.

The case came before this Court on a motion for a new trial.

C. Parker and *Charles Borcherling, Jr.*, for plaintiff.

Joseph P. Bradley, for defendants.

BEASLEY, C. J.—The motion for a new trial in this case is rested on two grounds, viz.: first, that the proofs will not sustain an action at law; second, that the damages are excessive.

On the first of these heads the ground taken is, that at the time when the plaintiff became the Rector of this congregation, and also at the time of the transaction complained of, the congregation was not incorporated. From this fact it was urged that the title under the deed from Mr. Peck could not pass out of him for the want of a competent grantee to take it, and that the members of the congregation were in possession of these premises as tenants in common by sufferance, and that, consequently, such rights in the realty as ordinarily pass to the Rector under a regular organization, did not in the present case vest.

So far as the law has to do with the relationship of the Rector with his flock, such relationship is to be regarded as the effect of a contract.

What, then, is the agreement into which a congregation of this denomination of Christians enters upon the call of a Rector? So far as touches the matter in controversy, it plainly appears to be this: They offer to the Minister receiving the call such rights in their temporalities as by the Ecclesiastical law of their sect, belong to the office which is tendered. one of such rights being that of preaching on Sundays in the Church provided by the congregation. Such an offer, therefore, can have nothing to do with the title to the Church edifice. No matter in whom the title may reside, if the congregation has the use of the building, the Rector must of necessity have the right to partake in such use. The agreement is not, as the argument on the part of the defendants assumed, that the Rector is to possess this class of privileges in these temporalities of which the congregation is the absolute owner. But to the contrary, whatever place the congregation provide for the purpose of public worship in the Parish, into such place the Rector, by virtue of his office, has the right to enter in order to conduct such worship. I have failed, therefore, to perceive how the fact of title to the Church premises in question is to affect the legal result in this case. In the view which I take of the understanding between these parties, it cannot matter at all whether or not the congregation had any interest in these premises other than a right to the occupation of them for the purpose of Divine service on the Sunday of the expulsion; because, if on that occasion this building was the place set apart by the congregation for their religious exercises, then it necessarily follows that the plaintiff at that time, *virtute officii*, had the legal right to be present and to conduct the worship. But the case in reality is much stronger in favor of the plaintiff than this. This Church property was put into the possession of this congregation for their denominational uses by Mr. Peck, the owner of the fee; they had erected their Church upon it, and thus complied with the conditions of the grant; it is true the title at law was defective, but it is also true that their title in equity was complete. This Church, thus built, had been consecrated by the Bishop of the Diocese, and by institution, performed with all due Ecclesiastical formalities, the plaintiff had been placed in charge of the spiritual affairs of the Church; the congretion remained in full possession of the Church edifice, and neither Mr. Peck nor any one else called such possession in question. Under the circumstances, how is it possible that these defendants, who claim to be the representatives of the congregation, can deny the rights of the Rector as to these premises on the ground of the inferiority of their own title? Suppose we regard them as mere tenants at sufferance, will that fact enable them to put an end to the rights of the plaintiff in this property? If such were their position, the only effect would be to make both their own rights and those of the Rector dependant on the will of the owner of the land. But it certainly would be contrary to all principle to permit a party in possession of real property to grant an interest in it to another, and then defeat such interest on the ground of his own inability to make such grant. The rule that a party cannot derogate from his own grant is one of universal efficacy, and applies in a very direct manner to the present case. Nor is there anything in the suggestion that the usual rights touching the temporalities which vest in the Rector, could not be obtained by him in the present instance, on account of the imperfection of the Ecclesiastical

7

organization of this congregation. The imperfection relied
on was the absence of an incorporation. But the want of this
quality does not at all affect the rights and duties of pastor
and people towards each other; the effect of becoming incorporated is to facilitate the acquisition and transfer of
property, and to enable the congregation to be represented
in the Convention of the Diocese: Article V. of Constitution
of P. E. C. of Diocese of New Jersey. But, by the canonical law of this denomination of Christians, it is not necessary, in order to constitute a Church, that the congregation
should take the form of an incorporated body. Indeed, the
very law of this State, which provides for the incorporation
of this class of churches, presupposes and requires that there
shall be antecedent to the inception of proceedings "a congregation of the Protestant Episcopal Church in this State
duly organized, according to the constitution and usages of
said church:" Act of 1829. In the case now before us, it
plainly appears that this Church was constituted in conformity to the Ecclesiastical law and usages applicable to it;
and the consequence is, that the plaintiff, by his official connection with it, acquired all the customary powers and
privileges pertaining to the Rectorship.

But there was a second objection taken on the argument,
which was, that on the assumption of the existence of the
right of the Rector to the privileges claimed by him, still it
was said, an innovation or disturbance of such rights would
not constitute the ground of a suit at law.

I cannot yield my assent to this proposition. The nature
of the right in question forbids such a result. I think it is
clear that, in right of his office, a Rector, by force of the law
of this Church, has either the possession of the Church edifice,
or has a privilege which enables him to enter into it—such
privilege being in the nature of an easement. Mr. Murray
Hoffman, in his learned and interesting treatise on the law
of the Protestant Episcopal Church in the United States,
page 266, in remarking on the effect of the incorporation of
churches, states his views in these terms, viz.: "The title
then to the church and all church property is in the trustees,
collectively, for all corporate purposes; but there is another

class of purposes purely Ecclesiastical, as to which the statute did not mean to interfere or prescribe any rule. These are to be controlled by the law of the church." And the conclusion to which he comes is thus stated : "That the control and possession of the Church edifice upon Sundays, and at all times when open for Divine services, appertains exclusively to the Rector." I have no doubt with regard to the correctness of this view. By the English Ecclesiastical law, which, although somewhat modified by new circumstances and by American usages and statutes, constitutes the substantial basis of the law controlling the affairs of this particular Church, the possession of the Church and churchyard is in the incumbent ; nor does it make any difference in' this respect, in whose hands the title to the religious property is lodged, as for example, in case the freehold of the Church and churchyard is in the Rector, nevertheless, the curate will be deemed in possession for all Ecclesiastical purposes. In exemplification of this rule, I refer to an interesting discussion of the question in *Greenslade* v. *Darby*, decided during the present year by the Court of Queen's Bench, Law Rep. 3 Q. B. 421. "I quite agree with the former decisions." Such is the declaration of Chief Justice Cockburn, that an incumbent has possession of the churchyard as well as of the Church for all spiritual purposes ; therefore for burials, and for all purposes attached to his office, he has undoubtedly uncontrolled possession of the churchyard. To the same purpose is the rule laid down by Cripps in his treatise on the Church and Clergy, page 158. See, also, 1 Burns' Ecclesiastical Law, 377 ; *Stocks* v. *Booth*, 1 T. R. 428. If, then, we adopt this theory, and I perceive no reason for rejecting it, that for the purpose of the exercise of his sacerdotal functions, the Rector becomes possessed of the Church buildings and grounds, it will be difficult to devise any pretext in denial of the right of such officer to a civil remedy if such possession be invaded. Nor does the right to redress for an interference with his rights, seem less clear, if we adopt the hypothesis, that by force of his position the plaintiff was possessed of an easement in these premises. Such a privilege would not be unlike in kind to a right to the occupation of a pew in a Church ;

and of this latter right in the case of *The Presbyterian Church*
v. *Andruss*, 1 Zabriskie 328, Chief Justice Green remarks, it
" is an incorporeal hereditament. It is in the nature of an
easement, a right or privilege in the lands of another. For
an interruption of this right, an action on the case for a disturbance, as in other cases of injury to incorporeal hereditaments, is the only remedy." Regarding, then, the Rector's
interest in the Church edifice as a mere right to enter, and
while there to discharge certain functions, I am unable to
distinguish it, in its substantial essence, from the right of the
pew holder. The right of the latter is obviously no more
secular in its character than the former; both the pew-holder
and the Minister attend to the end of religious worship and
edification, and as the pew-holder has a remedy at law for a
disturbance of his privilege, it would seem to be preposterous
to deny it to a Minister for a like wrong. Upon principle,
then, I think, the present action is to be vindicated, and for
a precedent I refer to the case of *Phillybrowne* v. *Ryland*, 3
Mod. 352, 2 Strange 624, in which it was decided that an
action would lie on behalf of a Parish over against the clerk
of the Vestry, for shutting the Vestry-door and keeping the
plaintiff out, so that he could not come in to vote. The rule
of decision in this case appears to be indistinguishable from
that which is called for by the one now before us.

Adopting, therefore, either of the views above indicated,
viz., that the plaintiff was in possession, or that he had a
right to enter on special occasions, the interference with
either of such interests affords a right of suit ; the mere fact
that the form of action would be variant if we adopt one or
the other theory, cannot affect this case on the present motion,
as the real question in controversy between the parties has
been tried, and consequently by force of the provision of our
present Practice Act, the mode of suit is now alterable, so as
to conform to the legal view which the Court may adopt.

Influenced by these considerations, I have concluded that
the plaintiff's right of action is sustained by the proofs in the
case.

On the second head my judgment is also in favor of the
plaintiff; the damages are undoubtedly large, but this ques-

tion was left fairly to the jury, and there is no reason to suppose that they were in any respect subjected to any sinister influence. The defendants acted with great indiscretion; their conduct was oppressive, and whatever their intentions may have been, it was calculated to wound and injure the plaintiff.

The verdict should not be disturbed.

APPENDIX II.

The case of the Rev. MILTON C. LIGHTNER, Rector of St. Paul's Church, Detroit, Michigan.

Shortly after the Easter election in the year 1866, it was found that the Vestry, which was composed of old and new members, were unanimous in their desire to get rid of the Rector of the Church. They met and passed resolutions of dismissal, and referred them to the Bishop for his concurrence. Thereupon the congregation rose and took steps to prevent the Vestry from carrying out their designs. They immediately prepared a letter of confidence in their Rector, which was signed by a large majority of them. It was intended to present it to the Vestry, but this was not done, as they had already informed the congregation that they did not hold themselves amenable to them, upon the ground that "ours is not a Congregational Church." The Bishop also expressed similar views. The paper, however, was sent to the Bishop, time having been allowed them before he acted, together with a letter requesting him to avert the calamity hanging over them.

The congregation thought the Church "Congregational" to the extent of there being a congregation recognized by its constitution; and warned of the antagonism of the Bishop to the Rector, they determined to move in their own self-defence, and instituted measures to hold another election, on the ground of the election of the Vestry having been irregular and unlawful. Notice of this election was read from the

chancel on Sunday, the 26th of August, and would have
been repeated on the next Sunday, but the Bishop, *who had
called together his Standing Committee* on the 23d of August,
and adjourned them to the 3d of September, got them together on the 29th of August, and on the next day Mr.
Lightner received the following letter:

DETROIT, *August* 30, 1866.
REV. M. C. LIGHTNER,

SIR:—I am instructed to inform you that you have been
dismissed from the Rectorship of St. Paul's Church, in the
city of Detroit, and that the Ecclesiastical authority of the
Diocese of Michigan has concurred in such dismissal; and to
notify you henceforth to refrain from using the Church building. I am also instructed to inform you that if you desire
to remain for the present in the parsonage house, you can
do so until it is needed for a new Rector, free of charge. I
enclose the sum of $208.33, which would have been due to
you, had your incumbency continued until October 1st.
B. VERNOR,
Secretary Vestry, St. Paul's Church, Detroit.

On the 6th of September, the day when the new election
was to be held, the congregation repaired to the Church, but
they found the doors locked and barricaded. The election
was held upon the sidewalk, and resulted in the choice of
two Wardens and eight Vestrymen as required by the Charter. (The objection to the Easter election was that ten Vestrymen and no Wardens were elected, and that this rendered
the election illegal and void.) The old Vestry held on to
their positions, whereupon a writ of *quo warranto* was issued
against them. Upon their demurrer to the information,
judgment was rendered in their favor.

Mr. Lightner, as late as March, 1867, remained in possession of the rectory, retained the Parish register, and performed the duties of his office outside of the Church edifice,
from which he was excluded by force. He filed a protest
with the Bishop against the interference by any other Minister with his rights and prerogatives as Rector of St. Paul's

Church. He also took counsel upon his rights in the matter, and received the following replies:

PHILADELPHIA, *December*, 31, 1866.

REV. M. C. LIGHTNER,
Detroit, Michigan:

I am clearly of the opinion that a Vestry has no right to dismiss a Rector, and thus dissolve the pastoral relation, without accusation or trial; and further, I am of opinion that any accusation or trial must be in accordance with the Ecclesiastical law of the communion to which the parties belong.

The legislation of 1865 prevents the dismissal of a Minister by a Vestry, with the assent of the Bishop, from being uncanonical, and relieves the parties from the penalties of the canon. I do not think, however, that it makes good a dismissal of the Rector without accusation or trial; or that it dissolves the contract between him and the Parish. Such a result would be in violation of general principles; and, I think, therefore, that the law of 1865 should be construed in subordination to these.

I give this opinion, with a saving of what the law of Michigan or the Charter of the Church may prescribe. I have not seen either of them.

Very sincerely and respectfully yours,

G. M. WHARTON.

PHILADELPHIA, *March* 18, 1867.

THE REV. MILTON C. LIGHTNER,

REV. AND DEAR SIR:—I have before me your request for a written opinion upon "the right of a Vestry to dismiss a Rector without accusation or trial." With the facts in any particular case which you may have in your mind, I am unacquainted; and if it were otherwise I should be reluctant to meddle, unless it were made my official duty. In what I shall say, therefore, I wish to be understood as dealing with an abstract question.

In Canon 4, of Title II., which is the only one contained in the Digest, bearing on the subject " Of the dissolution of a pastoral connection," it may be observed that a Minister *regularly settled* in a Parish or Church, is brought under the same provision as one *regularly instituted*, from which use of terms, I would understand that the Church in these United States, regards a Minister when settled as having the same rights and duties and occupying the same status before the law as when *instituted*.

Turning then to the " Office of Institution " in the prescribed Letter of Institution, we find it provided that due notice of a wish on either part to dissolve the sacerdotal relation between the Minister and the congregation, is to be given to the Bishop; and in case of any difference between the parties as to a separation, the Bishop with the advice of his Presbyters is to be the ultimate arbiter and judge.

Let me here take occasion to say, that the Prayer Book is of higher authority than the Canons, and that they are rather to be interpreted by it than it by them. The " Ecclesiastical authority," which is to take cognizance of the dissolution of a pastoral connection, is, we learn from the " Institution Office," not the Bishop alone, but the Bishop and his Presbyters, and they are to proceed in the consideration of any case, after the ways directed and obviously implied in the Letter of Institution. That this is indeed so appears from the history of our legislation.

The " Office of Institution " was adopted in 1804, and set forth with alterations in 1808. Simultaneously was adopted a canon, (modified also in 1808,) entitled " Of Difference between Ministers and their Congregations," and which begins with the following language : " In cases of controversy between Ministers who now and may hereafter hold the Rectorship of Churches or Parishes," etc. This canon provides that application shall be made by one or both the parties to the Bishop of the Diocese, and that he shall summon all the Presbyters of the Diocese ; and that if it shall appear to the Bishop and a majority of the Presbyters assembled, after such general summons, that the differences are irreconcilable, and that a dissolution of the connection is indispensably necessary, he and his said Presbyters shall recommend to said Ministers to relinquish their titles, on such conditions as may appear reasonable and proper to the Bishop, etc. Now it is evident that the Canon and the Office of Institution, were fash oned in conformity with one another, and that the Canon gives to Ministers who "hold Rectorships," the same protection which the officer gives to the Instituted. In both it is contemplated that the matter of difference between a Minister and a congregation, shall be considered by the Bishop and his Presbyters, with a view, if possible, to reconcilement; and that the separation, if it takes place, shall do so in conformity to their recommendation and on terms prescribed by them.

All this implied investigation involves the appearance of both parties before the Ecclesiastical tribunal. Indeed if there were no such implication, the settled principle of justice, which now obtains in all civilized countries, would require that before a man be condemned and suffer harm, he stand before the Court face to face with his accusers, and enjoy the opportunity to hear; and, if he can, refute their allegations.

I know it may be said that the canon to which I have referred was repealed by Canon 2 of Title IV. of the Digest. In point of fact it was, but in the intention of the General Convention *it was not*.* In 1856 a committee was appointed to prepare a Digest of all the Canon law of the Protestant Episcopal Church ; that is, to codify, arrange and harmonize existing laws—not to make any, not to expunge any. At the General Convention of 1859, that committee made its report. Preliminary to their recommendation that the Digest be adopted, they gave in their report the following assurances : " *The committee have also from a minute comparison satisfied themselves that no part of existing canons have been omitted.*"

The General Convention proceeded to accept and credit the Digest on the assurance thus given, that it contained every distinct provision which had been up to that moment in the canon law of the Church.

* Dr. Howe has since stated that he was in error on this point, although it in no way invalidates or weakens his argument.

94

If the features of the canon "Of differences between Ministers and their congregations," are not to be found in the Digest, they have been unwittingly omitted. The Church has never determined to repeal them.

However the question of their binding force might be settled by a civil Court, I think I have shown by a reference to the canon which contained them, and the contemporaneous language of the Office of Institution, that the bonds *declared* in that office, are in the Church regarded as inhering in the relation of a settled Minister and his congregation, and that neither party can dissolve the connection without consent of the other; that in case of differences, the matter must be brought before the Bishop; that he must convene a Council of Presbyters to consider with him *before the fact*, the expediency of separation; that they must effect reconciliation if possible, and if not, determine terms and conditions of dissolution, which the parties must, under penalty, accept.

To make this process just, it is indispensable that the contestants appear face to face before the proper tribunal.

And without these conditions any attempted severance of the pastoral relation by one of the parties to it, contrary to the will of the other, is against the good order of the Church, besides being a violation of the common law in all constitutional government—that no man shall be condemned unheard. Local diocesan canons may differ in detail from the canons of the general Church. In what I have written I have not taken them into account.

If every Rector were removable at the caprice of his Vestry, sanctioned by an *ex parte* presentation of their case before the Bishop, we should be in a pitiable condition.

Very truly,

Your brother in Christ.

M. A. DE WOLFE HOWE.

APPENDIX III.

A statement of the case of the Rev. WILLIAM RAWLINS PICKMAN, Rector of St. Peter's Church, Salem, Massachusetts. Mr. Pickman was Rector of St. Peter's Church, and on April 18th, 1865, received the following communication:

EASTER TUESDAY, *April* 18, 1865.

REV. AND DEAR SIR:—At the annual Easter meeting last evening, the following resolutions were passed by a vote of thirty-four yeas to fifteen nays.

" *Resolved*, That the proprietors of St. Peter's Church, in Parish meeting assembled, feel constrained to express their opinion and conviction that the interests of the Parish will be best subserved by a termination of the connection between them and their present Rector.

" *Resolved*, That the clerk cause a copy of these resolutions to be sent to Rev. Mr. Pickman, and that when this meeting adjourn, it adjourn to meet at this place on Monday evening next at 7½ o'clock P. M."

To this the Rector replied, that were he " to accede to their resolution, he would go from them with an utterly ruined character;" that while he " had been assailed by public slander with a grossness, a pertinacity, and a malignity which falls to the lot of few men," they had refused, as a body, to bring any charges against him, by meeting which he could defend himself, and that in short he " felt constrained to express his ' opinion and conviction,' that the interests of the Parish and the interests of the Rector would be materially injured by a termination of the connection existing between them at present."

At a subsequent meeting of the " proprietors," the following resolution was passed by a vote of thirty-seven to eight.

" *Resolved*, That for the purpose of bringing back harmony to the Parish, and wholly disclaiming any intention of imputing to the Rector any wrong, the proprietors hereby reiterate their opinion as to the expediency and necessity of such dissolution, and most respectfully and earnestly request their Rector, the Rev. Wm. Rawlins Pickman, to resign his charge of this Parish."

The Rector declining to follow the advice of these gentlemen, at a subsequent meeting, by a vote of thirty-seven to nine, they declared the pastoral relation dissolved, and appointed a committee "to apply at once to the Bishop for his concurrence in such dissolution."

The application having been made, the Bishop replied to the chairman of the committee as follows:

Boston, *May* 10, 1865.

My Dear Sir :—I have received from you a copy of certain proceedings of the proprietors of St. Peter's Church, Salem, including a resolution which was passed dissolving the pastoral relations between the Parish and its Rector, and appointing a committee to ask for my concurrence in such dissolution. You also, on behalf of said committee, request me to indicate the time, place and mode in which it will please me to meet the committee, and hear their views on the subject.

Having already heard statements from two gentlemen of St. Peter's, in a recent visit which they made to me, and also stated my views to them, I do not perceive the necessity of a personal conference with the committee. In one of the resolutions passed on May 1st, the proprietors declare that, in one resolution adopted in the annual Easter meeting, they had " no purpose of casting any imputation upon the character of their Rector in any of his relations as a man, a clergyman, or a Christian," and in the other resolution they wholly disclaim "any intention of imputing to the Rector any wrong."

This being the statement of the proprietors in regard to the Rev. Mr. Pickman, *I feel that I should do a great act of injustice to him*, by concurring with the action of the proprietors. I therefore decline so doing.

I am very respectfully yours,

MANTON EASTBURN.

John Kilburn.

APPENDIX IV.

The case of the Rev. LIBERTUS VAN BOKKELEN, D. D., Rector of St. Timothy's Church, Catonsville, Baltimore county, Maryland.

On Easter Monday, 1871, an election was held in this Church, for members of the Vestry. The result caused great dissatisfaction in the Church, being brought about, as it was alleged, by the votes of persons who were neither members of nor communicants at that Church, and some of whom were members of other churches. It was also alleged that some of the Vestrymen elected were ineligible to the office for the same reasons. On April 24th, 1871, the Vestry met, and a motion was offered proposing to declare the Rectorship of St. Timothy's Church vacant, on and after May 1st. This the Rector ruled out of order, and declined to call the vote upon it. The Register then demanded the yeas, to which some persons responded. The nays were not called, nor was the result of the vote declared, the persons present, and the Rector, leaving the room instantly, without the formality of an adjournment. It was alleged that this was the work of a *few* against *many* in the congregation. On May 1st, 1871, the Register and Wardens demanded of the Rector, the keys of the Church, and all the Church property in his hands. This demand he refused to comply with, and stated that he could not recognize the right to interfere with his duty as a settled Rector, nor did he believe them to represent the will of the congregation, by which, clearly expressed, he was ready to abide. On this same day, a meeting of the congregation was held, at which the Rector stated the above facts, and appealed to them to know their will. It was by them unanimously

Resolved, That the congregation of St. Timothy's Church, approve and endorse the action of their Rector, in refusing to give up the keys of the Church, or to relinquish his control over any portion of the Church property, committed to his care; and we direct him to retain possession of the same as heretofore.

Also, resolved, That we recognize him as the Rector of St. Timothy's Church, and approve his decision to continue the discharge of the duties of his office, and advise him not to regard the action of persons who do not represent our will, and, by their conduct, prove themselves not to be exponents of the wishes or interests of the Church.

It was also resolved, That a committee be appointed to lay all the facts before the Bishop of the Diocese, and to ask his interposition and paternal counsel.

The Vestry also prepared a statement of the case, and the action taken by them, and submitted it to the Bishop.

The Bishop replied to their communication as follows:

MADISON SQUARE, *May* 10, 1871.

DAVID FOWLER, ESQ.,

MY DEAR SIR:—I have given my best attention to the paper bearing your signature, with others, which I yesterday received through the kind attention of Mr. F. W. Brune, and about which you and I have had some conversation at our casual meeting in the street.

Remembering the tenor of remarks which then fell from you, I know that you will be surprised to learn, that I find your case less strongly put, as regards numbers, in your statements, than I had been led to expect by the partial investigation I had already made.

Of the proceedings of the Vestry elected on Easter Monday, I had also been informed, in exact accordance with your account, and with rather more particularity.

But your account of the measures taken by those dissatisfied with the proceedings in question, is less accurate, both as to their form and tendency, and as to their grounds.

I understand them to question the legality of the election of the present claimants to be a Vestry—not on any ground of irregularity or informality in the election, but on the ground of insufficient qualification, both of some of the persons admitted to vote, and of some of the persons chosen to be Vestrymen.

If either of the latter were an unbaptized, non-communicant person, or, being a baptized person, were at the time of his election, actually a member of a Board of Trustees of another religious denomination, such choice was undoubtedly invalid, by the terms of the Constitution of St. Timothy's Church, as I understand them.

But it does not appertain to my office to decide the question of legality; which I may, nevertheless, have a clear opinion as to the question of propriety.

The opposition to the action of the body claiming to be the Vestry, was based on grounds quite independent of the question of legal election. The powers of the Vestry being derived from the Constitution, does not extend to such action, as you state the majority of the Vestry to have attempted to take by a resolution for the removal of the Rector. The position of that officer of the Church cannot be affected by any action of the Vestry, subsequent to his election, under the Constitution.

It is a consequence of the powerlessness of the Vestry to remove a Rector, that no action of that body can effect the right of a Rector to receive all contributions for his support, or of individual members of the congregation to make and collect such contributions. Any resolution of the Vestry about contract with the Rector, can only affect the liability of the body as a Corporation.

The occupation of a Rectory is a consequence of the tenure of Rectorship, unless stipulation to the contrary was made and agreed to at the time of election.

On these grounds I understand the opponents of your measures to base their determination to continue the recognition of the present incumbent of St. Timothy's Church as the lawful Rector, entitled to the occupancy of the Rectory, and the receipt of all contributions made for the support of the ministry in the Church, and the exercise of all canonical functions and rights pertaining to the Rector's office.

As at present informed, I cannot regard their determination otherwise than as well taken.

I think it right, in this connection, to state to you that after considering a memorial presented to the Rev. Dr. Van

Bokkelen, with the signatures of a larger number of the members of the congregation of St. Timothy's Church than are claimed to be disposed to concur in your statement, and conferring upon the subject of its contents and signatures with the highlyr espectable delegation, which laid it before me, I deemed myself bound to give my official opinion unfavorably in relation to any proposal of resignation of the Rectorship.

As informed both by that document and conference, and by the remarkable extent to which I find them corroborated by the contents of your statement, I cannot but be of opinion that the Rector of St. Timothy's owes it to the rights of the majority of the congregation for which he ministers, and to his own obligation to maintain inviolate the established order o. the Church of which he is a Minister, not to forsake his position without other and more sufficient grounds for vacating it than have as yet been made apparent.

Permit me, in conclusion, to take the liberty of suggesting, that if the numerous and respectable body of persons, attested in the list appended to your document to be ready and desirous to become pew-holders in St. Timothy's Church, but unable to do so for want of harmony with Dr. Van Bokkelen and his friends, should be found able and willing to unite in the support of ministrations more agreeable to their own sense of need and fitness, they are amply sufficient to organize, under leave of the Convention of the Diocese, a congregation, in which it would be in their power to regulate matters in accordance with their own views, while the rapidly increasing population and prosperity of that part of Baltimore county, would make the provision of an additional Church so set on foot, highly seasonable and commendable, provided the discretion to be expected were exercised in the choice of a locality.

I am, dear sir, with affectionate regard,

Your faithful friend and servant,

WILLIAM R. WHITINGHAM,

Bishop of Maryland.

www.ingramcontent.com/pod-product-compliance
Lightning Source LLC
Chambersburg PA
CBHW032358280326
41935CB00008B/620

*9 7 8 3 3 3 7 8 1 5 9 2 9 *